17 Aug. 2021

The Invitation

Dear Larry + Phyllis,

Thank you so much for your hospitality during my recent visit to Chicago with my dad.

Among other things I write some poetry. I hope you might enjoy them.

Brian :)

Aug. 2001

Dear Lawrence + Phyllis,

Thank you so much for your hospitality during my recent visit to Chicago with my dad.

Among other things I wrote some poetry. I hope you might enjoy these.

Thanks!!

The Invitation

365 Selections from Brian's Poem of the Day
(Vol. 4)

Brian J. Mueller

Bound Poetry Books

by Brian J. Mueller
is licensed under a Creative Commons
Attribution-NonCommercial-NoDerivatives 4.0 International License.

Permissions beyond the scope of this license may be available at
https://www.brianspoems.com.

Cover Design Inspired by Christine Horner
The Book Cover Whisperer

Contents

Dedication
19

Introduction
23

January
25

February
65

March
99

April
135

May
175

June
215

July
253

August
291

September
325

October
357

November
393

December
427

Acknowledgements
461

About Brian
462

Also by Brian J. Mueller
463

Notes
464

JANUARY

SUN	MON	TUE	WED	THU	FRI	SAT
			1 It's in the Stillness	2 Essential Truth #1	3 Essenial Truth #2	4 Essential Truth #3
5 Essential Truth #4	6 Essential Truth #5	7 Keeping Awake	8 Tuning	9 A Call to Relax	10 Along a River	11 Let's Move
12 Nighttime	13 Your Heartbeat	14 Here With Me	15 The Call of Duty	16 Oh My Heart	17 Growing Pains	18 While at Peace
19 Confessions	20 The Pathless Path	21 The Right Questions	22 In Exile	23 After the Curtain	24 It's All Right	25 The Heart of the Matter
26 Right Now	27 The Market Mindset	28 The First Line	29 Serenity Salesmen	30 Don't Make it Worse	31 Donny Football	

FEBRUARY

SUN	MON	TUE	WED	THU	FRI	SAT
						1 The Invitation
2 The Only Way to Get There	3 With Arms Wide	4 Within Himself	5 Under-standing Avenue	6 Go Deep	7 A Healing Light	8 A Place to Always
9 Before Bed	10 Revisiting the Flow	11 How Silly	12 Bit O' Gold	13 Sing Along	14 Be Patient	15 How to Forget
16 The Silent Songs	17 Calendar App	18 It's in the Middles	19 Reclama-tion	20 Life Demands	21 Forever	22 New Meaning
23 Bleeding	24 Accept the Call	25 All Goes Away	26 In the Dirt	27 Now I Know	28 River Wisdom	29 River Return

MARCH

SUN	MON	TUE	WED	THU	FRI	SAT
1 Quantum Mechanics	2 A Time to Rest	3 The Walls	4 There's Still Time	5 I Am Overcome	6 The Veil Lifted	7 Impərfəct Lovə
8 Growing Space	9 My Plans	10 Wise Counsel	11 Truth	12 My Screens	13 How I Love	14 Slow Dancing
15 Life Is Fine	16 Do Something	17 Go Out and Play	18 Tiny Arrows	19 The Blue Pill	20 My Own Worst Enemy	21 Circles
22 Tenderness	23 Don't Buy More Clothes	24 Becoming Speechless	25 His Mother	26 Prickly People	27 Onions	28 Giving Myself
29 Acquiescence	30 Immigrant Song	31 Time is Relative				

APRIL

SUN	MON	TUE	WED	THU	FRI	SAT
			1 Just Let It Happen	2 A Seed	3 A Good Seat	4 Start Listening
5 Inundated	6 Pray Constantly	7 Right Here, Right Now	8 Ice Age Truth	9 Lighten Your Load	10 Once You See	11 Lightness of Being
12 Exposed	13 Last Night	14 Approach God	15 It's So Easy	16 Belly Fat	17 You Won't Be President	18 Us
19 Here and Everywhere	20 An Artist's Prayer	21 Dark Was the Night	22 The Infinitude	23 The Path of Descent	24 Jubilee	25 Learning to Fly
26 The Virus	27 Feel the Weight	28 Keep Your Pennies	29 Emptiness	30 Should I Be Worried?		

MAY

SUN	MON	TUE	WED	THU	FRI	SAT
					1 We Can't Go Back	2 Would You Change
3 Imperfection	4 Bullshit Jobs	5 My Fast	6 Only My Soul (The Way Is Love)	7 When All This Is Over	8 Bellyache	9 Joker
10 Off-Center	11 Divine Riddles	12 What Else	13 To Ash, To Dust	14 The More I Learn	15 As I Understand	16 Until Now
17 Moon Hanging	18 Money Confusion	19 Zombies	20 Headlong	21 Firmly Grounded	22 We Only See	23 Bedeviled
24 One Life	25 We're All in This	26 The Eternal Journey	27 Politics	28 Our Cells	29 Try Not to Forget	30 I Had to Divorce
31 My Soul Lifts						

JUNE

SUN	MON	TUE	WED	THU	FRI	SAT
	1 Around the Bend	2 Newton's Cradle	3 Preacher Man	4 Be Released	5 A Good Sign	6 Reverence Falls
7 Hunted	8 A Long Relationship	9 Show Up	10 What I'd Say	11 I Need You	12 Empty Cupboards	13 With No Wind
14 Compassion	15 Testify!	16 Wrong or Right	17 A Little Suffering	18 A Love Letter	19 Save Me	20 Doing Less
21 Your Anger	22 Tempting Fate	23 Not Voting	24 I Keep on Writing	25 The Specialist	26 My Life Story	27 The Perfect Space
28 Change of Heart	29 Morning Bell	30 Stolen Voice				

JULY

SUN	MON	TUE	WED	THU	FRI	SAT
			1 Weary Confession	2 Hesitating Beauty	3 Little Bitty Me	4 Socialism
5 Pandemic	6 The Gears	7 Falling Slowly	8 DNR	9 34	10 Shock Doctrine	11 You Don't Notice
12 Inside the Lines	13 Sacred Seeds	14 Tinkerer	15 Cassandra Complex	16 Wanting to Escape	17 The Panic Ends	18 Enjoy the Silence
19 A Point of View	20 Love Changes	21 Like a Rock	22 Unitive Love	23 Grace	24 My Grief	25 Sobriety
26 A Toothache	27 Sinusitis	28 Crawly Things	29 What Feeds Me	30 Good Fortune	31 What Beckons	

AUGUST

SUN	MON	TUE	WED	THU	FRI	SAT
					1 My Laundry List	2 Over and Again
3 The Sound of Silence	4 At the Creek Bottom	5 Sing	6 Saltwater	7 Healing Modalities	8 The Notes	9 Community
10 Releasing	11 Tell Me	12 Take That Leap	13 Joy of Being	14 Bite Your Tongue	15 A Beginning's End	16 The Silver Lining
17 Beyond Cost	18 The Manuals	19 Nothing Beyond Living	20 Come into the Light	21 Truth and the Soul	22 Figuring It All Out	23 Churched
24 She 31 Cheers to the Misfits!	25 Presbyopia	26 Those Who Survive	27 Witness Me Bargaining	28 What's the Right Amount?	29 A Prayer for Everyone	30 Twice

SEPTEMBER

SUN	MON	TUE	WED	THU	FRI	SAT
	1 Set Yourself Free	2 Rock	3 Love	4 Harmony	5 The Winds	6 Nostalgia
7 Lucky	8 Decay	9 Soul Food	10 Awakened	11 The Poetry of Fierce Landscapes	12 If Ever...	13 The Crescendo
14 All Those Places	15 I Used to Know	16 A Softening	17 Grand-father	18 Amazing Grace	19 Things I Don't Remember	20 Surprising
21 Silencio	22 To Be an X	23 My Soul Is Serene	24 Instrument of Love	25 My First Poem	26 Beyond Love Stories	27 Breath
28 Manhood	29 Pour	30 The Real Thing				

OCTOBER

SUN	MON	TUE	WED	THU	FRI	SAT
			1 Outages	2 Love Is	3 Intimacy	4 We Belong
5 For All Those Days	6 Stars Are the Light	7 Beating Heart	8 Foot Rub	9 This Sacred Space	10 My Favorite Colors	11 A Love Feast
12 Oblivion	13 Decoding the Spirits	14 Everyone	15 A Better Me	16 Impermanence	17 Timeless Truth	18 Birkenstock
19 Did Not Last	20 Inner Peace	21 Who Am I Kidding?	22 Oh, Grow Up!	23 What Am I Doing?	24 Memories	25 Adoption Day
26 Here and Now	27 Fix Everything	28 Other People's Feelings	29 As Water Goes	30 Divine Mystery	31 Go Ahead, Cry	

NOVEMBER

SUN	MON	TUE	WED	THU	FRI	SAT
						1 Here All Along
2 Pull the Plug	3 Before I Begin...	4 So Simple	5 Guy Fawkes	6 Source to Mouth	7 Great Conversations	8 Overcome
9 A Bigger Fight	10 It's Not Time	11 Call to Your Soul	12 Second Spring	13 Fold 'em	14 A Slave Ship Called Jesus	15 Musical Chairs
16 Always Remember	17 Conformity	18 For What It's Worth	19 Rock in My Shoe	20 Little Me	21 Winter Weather	22 The Fixers
23 A Great Awakening 30 Responsibility	24 Sacred Reasons	25 Baked	26 Numb	27 Cults	28 Recklessness	29 Relax

DECEMBER

SUN	MON	TUE	WED	THU	FRI	SAT
	1 No Signal	2 Soul Talk	3 Tick of the Clock	4 The Appalachians	5 Maybe	6 At Home
7 A Day Off	8 Brian Shrugged	9 One and the Same	10 We're All Poets	11 Trusting Uncertainty	12 Lost in Presidio	13 Listen from the Heart
14 Speak from the Heart	15 Be Spontaneous and Authentic	16 Be Lean of Expression	17 Tilt Tenderly	18 Rest Assured	19 Some Reason	20 Remembering
21 Fire and Ice	22 Drifting	23 Immortality	24 Born Again	25 Year End	26 A Blessing	27 Falling Water
28 Peace Now	29 A Free Lunch	30 Clearheaded	31 Getting Past the Past			

Dedication

I'd like to dedicate this book to Bob F., Bob S., Charlie, Chuck R., Chuck S., Dan R., Dan V., Doug, Earl, Ed, Herb, Jes, Jim, John, Mick, Shawn, Rich, Ron, Tom S., Tom S., Shawn, my Dad, and all the other men in Ohio and elsewhere who come together in what we call men's work with the stated commitment to help each other become better and more authentic men.

You can learn more about our efforts to support men on a spiritual journey at OhioIlluman.org / Illuman.org. We welcome all men to our work without regard for ethnicity, class, education, sexual orientation, religion or any other characteristic that might make them feel excluded.

Experience the Power of a Poem!™

*I know all my poems come from a wanting to give
something useful.*
    ~ Hafiz

*Why, when God's world is so big,
did you fall asleep in a prison of all places?*
    ~ Rumi

Introduction

Thank you for picking up the fourth volume of *Brian's Poem of the Day*. I hope the title caught your attention. The idea for it came to me about a year ago. At that time, it occurred to me we all receive countless invitations throughout our lives. In fact, I daresay our pockets are full of them right now, even though we don't realize it.

To be sure, we all receive invitations to make changes both big and small. Most of the time we get invitations and just ignore them, or never even see them as such. As I write these words, I'm thinking about a time in my life ten years or more ago when my first marriage was coming to an end, even though I just couldn't see it. I now recall receiving an invitation to stop making external changes in my life and to start seeking internal change and growth. Nevertheless, for some length of time I resisted this repeated invite to look inward.

Finally, there came a point when I had no other choice. In order to move forward in my life, I was going to have to accept that invitation to do some personal and spiritual work. Boy, was I surprised when I also discovered all the invitations I had discarded that were now strewn about me like litter along a pathway! For a while it made me angry that I was oblivious to what I needed to do. However, I now take solace through understanding most of us won't ever notice an invitation until we're truly ready to receive and act upon it.

Maybe it's a bit hubristic to say, but I hope in all these poems there's at least one that will come across as an invitation to you, or perhaps one that will remind you of an invitation that you too have received. As I continue along on my own life journey, it's become clear that the invitations will never stop coming. Therefore, I pray we'll all be a little more open to accepting them when they arrive.

JANUARY

January 1

IT'S IN THE STILLNESS
...all the pieces come together.

Gather with you to the stillness
as much as you can carry.
Then allow it to spill over
into that abyss called forgetting.

The next morning you will awaken
with a reaffirmed sense of knowing,
but newly aware anything not pointing
to the absolute uncertainty called God
is no longer worth holding onto.

Other Voices

*Like colors on a painter's palette,
there's a mixture in the middle.
Sometimes the color you get
depends on the colors you have.*
~ Brian J. Mueller

January 2

ESSENTIAL TRUTH #1
Life is hard.

You probably don't remember when
you were first signed by the cross,
or marked in some other sacred way
to symbolize that life is hard.

Or maybe you remember it well,
that very first punch in the gut,
and have known ever since
life is bitter and difficult.

But even if you learned it late
because of some early good fortune,
experience removes all uncertainty
of life's pain and misery.

Remember this:
A hard day is a blessing.
An easy day is a blessing.

Every path that you choose,
or that will be chosen for you,
in due time affirms
both are true.

Other Voices

*If you would only recognize that life is hard,
things would be so much easier for you.*
~ Louis D. Brandeis

January 3

ESSENTIAL TRUTH #2
You are going to die.

    Make believe is for children
    who are trying on the many roles
    they may decide to wear
    on their journey through life.

    But you don't need to pretend.
    For better or worse you know
    exactly who you are
    and who you aren't.
    You have taken stock
    of your successes and regrets.

    You may love children,
    including the one you once were,
    but you can no longer make believe
    the life you know is infinite
    and will go with you
    into eternity.

    A child looks upon an empty horizon,
    but you see a ship fast approaching.

    One day soon,
    you will take your sacred wounds
    and board this ship on a voyage
    through and beyond death,
    into new life.

Other Voices

*The day which we fear as our last
is but the birthday of eternity.*
~ Lucius Annaeus Seneca

January 4

ESSENTIAL TRUTH #3
You are not that important.

It was probably a man,
one you knew and loved,
who was the first to inform you
you're not that important.

Maybe he did so angrily,
shouting inches from your face.
Or maybe he did so passively,
by disappearing without a trace.

Or perhaps I'm wrong
and it was someone
or something else entirely
who first pulled the wool
away from your eyes.

By now you've spent
all these years searching
and building your life using
a reputation, a job, a family,
something - anything
in order to show everyone,
especially that person
staring at you in the mirror,
how important you are.

It can work for a while,
but life is nefarious
and has many ways
to empty us of self.

As you now turn
toward the journey home,
back to who you truly are,
you will find a great peace

not in your worthiness,
but in those twin abilities
called forgiveness and love,
forever emanating from
your beating heart.

Other Voices

*Nearly everything you do is of no importance,
but it is important that you do it.*
~ Mahatma Gandhi

January 5

ESSENTIAL TRUTH #4
You are not in control.

Tell me how
and tell me when
you first realized
you are not in control.

Was it that awful day
you had something treasured
stolen away from you?

Or was it the day
you asked a question
and received no answer?

Maybe it was the time
you learned what is meant
by the word inevitability.

For some it comes wondrously,
that moment of absolute awe
after putting an eye to a telescope
and seeing our solar system
for the very first time.

For me it came with a bellyache
and was blown in on a dusty wind.

As I wiped the mud from my eyes
I began to feel a little better,
at last liberated from the yoke
of divine responsibility,
but still uneasy and learning to live
in my new found humility.

Other Voices

A journey is like marriage.
The certain way to be wrong is to think you control it.
- John Steinbeck

January 6

ESSENTIAL TRUTH #5
Your life is not about you.

Join me in a sigh.
I say join me in a sigh...

In this shrug is your acceptance,
your body's way of making peace
and at last receiving this message:
Your life is not about you.

Now that you know
you will see it everywhere,
everything alive and busily giving
body and soul for no reason
but in love of this world.

Do not feed the pain
you hold down deep inside.
Reverse the flow of energy
from within to without
thus freeing your mind,
your body and your soul,
to live in communion
with all things.

Other Voices

*Once we accept our limits,
we go beyond them.*
~ Albert Einstein

January 7

KEEPING AWAKE
through the suffering.

There is a kind of silence
that is full of noise,
and a kind of dryness
that is sopping wet.

So doesn't it follow
there might be a pain,
after which will exist
some unexpected joy?

I see the need for certainty.
How else could you build
a rocket to the moon?

But more relevant
to your life this coming day,
when the milk suddenly sours
and the truth you've been holding
rips through the brown paper sack
you've carried too long at your side,
is a gentle reminder to keep going
and not attempt to recover
whatever has been lost.

Remember all you can,
then continue your search
through pain and darkness
for a shining new light.

Other Voices

*Although the world is full of suffering,
it is also full of the overcoming of it.*
~ Helen Keller

January 8

TUNING
...into and beyond your life.

Tune.
Keep tuning.
Continue making
ever-finer adjustments.
You will notice the signal
gradually growing stronger
as the message becomes clearer,
gentler and more loving.

If at the culmination
of all your patient tuning
the only transmission you receive
is a profound and perfect silence,
be reassured by the tranquility.

At long last you've found
exactly what you've been seeking!

Other Voices

*I wash my hands of those
who imagine chattering to be knowledge,
silence to be ignorance,
and affection to be art.*
   ~ Kahlil Gibran

January 9

A CALL TO RELAX
...and be present to life.

I'm too quick to blame
a long day for my problems,
when more often it's just me
who's not getting the message.

Then I'll take my dog for a walk,
and in the trees I'll hear voices
lovingly urging me to relax
and be gentler with myself.

Afterwards I'm able to allow
those most delicate feelings
I once refused to acknowledge
to spill out over these pages.

Slowly I am learning:
Even amidst the chaos
there is plenty of patience,
courage, strength and love
for me to rely on.

Other Voices

*Why are there trees I never walk under
but large and melodious thoughts descend upon me?*
~ WALT WHITMAN

January 10

ALONG A RIVER
...your life flows toward you.

Upstream a flood fills this waterway,
and now the current is pushing,
pushing forth a river of debris.

In the swirling eddies of muddy water,
you see and identify many strange things.

Look!
It's a bicycle wheel but no bike.

There tumbles an old sofa!
But where are its cushions?

This river of debris is a reminder
of the way life surges toward you.
It carries within it the lives of others,
along with everything else it can find
not protected from the relentless gush,
forever heading downstream.

Other Voices

I was thinking:
so this is how you swim inward,
so this is how you flow outward,
so this is how you pray.
  ~ Mary Oliver, Five A.M. in the Pinewoods

January 11

LET'S MOVE
...or get out of the way!

Just as water seeks a level,
so too do the many forces
invisibly working in the world.

Our entire planet is balanced
between the light of day
and the dark of night.

It rests at the right temperature
from the sweltering Equator
to the frigid Antarctic.

It knows the right mixture
of oxygen to carbon dioxide,
salt to fresh water,
and desert to forest land.

Whenever imbalance disrupts
this energetic harmony
benevolent forces emerge
to both restore and recreate
the stabilizing mechanisms
which allow for a new equilibrium.

Sadly, it's just as natural
for forces to resist the call
to adapt and to change.

Yet when inevitability comes knocking,
everyone must find a way to move
or get the hell out of the way.

Other Voices

*Lead, follow,
or get out of the way.*
~ Unknown Origin

January 12

NIGHTTIME
...is so different from the day.

    Waking up at 2am
    to take Simon outside
    reveals a shadowy world
    I've never really known.

    The moon hangs higher
    and appears to shine brighter.
    The rooftops seem to be glowing,
    and I suspect a few of my neighbors
    are still sitting on their sofas,
    tuned in to the *Late Late Show*.

    Out in the street
    I notice something moving,
    but before I can find my light
    it disappears down a storm drain.

    We stumble back inside,
    and while removing his harness
    I sleepily grumble:

    Let's go back to sleep, Simon.
    In a few hours it'll be a different world.

Other Voices

Think in the morning.
Act in the noon.
Eat in the evening.
Sleep in the night.
    ~ William Blake

January 13

YOUR HEARTBEAT
...is like a blaze of light.

Has anyone ever asked you
what makes your heart beat?

Have you ever stopped to listen
to the rhythms your body makes
as you move through life?

Maybe it's love.
Maybe it's another potent emotion
feeding the ticktock beating
at the center of your being.

More likely it's magic,
or something we can only know
as magic or as God
or as a blaze of light
bursting through a crack
in our humanity.

No matter the mystery,
my heart keeps beating,
my heart keeps beating,
my heart keeps beating.

And I never think to ask why,
just as I never want it to stop.

Other Voices

*The goal of life is to make your heartbeat
match the beat of the universe,
to match your nature with Nature.*
~ JOSEPH CAMPBELL

January 14

HERE WITH ME
...for Ed

You could be anywhere,
but you're here with me.

Thank you,
thank you so much
for being here with me.

Your life is noisy.
Your life is busy.
Death came calling.
Fear came calling.
But you still showed up
to be here with me.

The wine in your cup,
the water in your eyes,
the silence surrounding you,
sanctifies your humble presence.

I'm so glad you're here with me.

Other Voices

We convince by our presence.
    ~ Walt Whitman

January 15

THE CALL OF DUTY
...is to love and be loved.

It's easier to fool a young man
with promises of immortality
and delusions of grandeur
than to convince him patience
will deliver him to a new life
through and beyond
the death he fears.

Give a man reason to die
and watch him do so gladly.

Offer a man a long life
in deep connection to his heart,
and the first time around
he'll always choose death.

Other Voices

*Sometime they'll give a war
and nobody will come.*
~ Carl Sandburg

January 16

OH MY HEART
...keeps pounding.

Who gets my heart pounding?

She
her
he
him
they
them
us
we

These are the people
who make my heart pound.

What gets my heart pounding?

Anticipation
expectation
hunger
eating, drinking, dancing
doing anything right now
being alone
or even better
being with you
but even
sadness
frustration
fear
and helplessness

All of these things
make my heart pound.

When does my heart pound?

When I'm alive
when I'm present
when I'm alone
when I'm afraid
when I'm in community
when I'm happy
when I'm unaware
when I'm breathing
when I'm holding my breath
when I'm inside you
when you're inside me

That's when my heart pounds.

Other Voices

Rhythm is sound in motion.
It is related to the pulse,
the heartbeat, the way we breathe.
It rises and falls.
It takes us into ourselves;
it takes us out of ourselves.
  ~ Edward Hirsch

January 17

GROWING PAINS
...never end

What stretches me?

Everything stretches me.

I say it again:
Everything stretches me.

Middle age
Growing older
Going on
Uncertainty
Marriage
Friendships
Dying
Living with death
Too much
Too little
Eating and drinking
And drinking
My lack of control
Having too much control
Winning
Losing
Forgetting
Remembering
Not being able to let go
Letting go of too much
Meaninglessness
No creativity
Emptiness
No limits
No sound
No light
No all of those things
that make me remember

I'm alive.

And at the end,
there being no end,
only beginning.

Other Voices

The key to growth is the introduction of higher dimensions of consciousness into our awareness.
    ~ Laozi

January 18

WHILE AT PEACE
...don't think too hard.

What brings me balance?

Breath
breath
breath
as many deep breaths
as I can take
before passing out

Tea
more tea

Melissa
and Simon

Remembering
what it's like
to be held by my parents
to be held in liminal space
to be held in the arms of God
where there is nothing
nothing to hold onto
nothing between me
and everything else
unique but made of
the same exact stuff:

love.

Other Voices

I balanced all,
brought all to mind,
the years to come seemed waste of breath,
a waste of breath the years behind,
in balance with this life,
this death.
  ~ WILLIAM BUTLER YEATS

January 19

CONFESSIONS
...are a place I call home.

I no longer care
who wins what,
how to get there,
when the right time is,
or the precise words to say
at that right time.

This is a poem about peace
and the price of that peace,
which I pay out gradually
with my flesh, blood and bones.

When I woke up yesterday
there was nothing more I could do
to deny my own pain and suffering.
And that's when I knew denying
is what I've been doing all along.

So I've made my confession,
and these words are now part
of my permanent record.

Let my next breath be
the beginning of a ritual,
which brings me back home
and restores my wholeness
in God and this Universe.

Other Voices

A confession has to be part of your new life.
~ LUDWIG WITTGENSTEIN

January 20

THE PATHLESS PATH
...for M.C.

As a child
I spoke to the world
and it spoke to me,
in ways I'd forgotten
until recently.

Along my journey
I never met a single tree,
toad, squirrel or swallow,
who mentioned retirement,
or would babble on and on
about rugged individualism.

And when tall mountains
would show me their fossils
and tell stories about living
deep beneath the ancient seas,
they never thought to mention
where they went to school
or their plans for the future.

Now, from afar,
a woman's voice needles me.
She says that we all think
we're on the road to somewhere,
when what we're really on
is the pathless path.

Other Voices

*I believe that all roads lead to the same place -
and that is wherever all roads lead to.*
~ Willie Nelson

January 21

THE RIGHT QUESTIONS
...will eventually arise.

The night air is crisp,
the dawn still an hour away.
A moth greets me at the door,
then floats silently beside us
into the moon shadows.

Simon does his business
at the bottom of the driveway,
so we quickly head back inside
to begin our daily routine.

Day to day,
hour to hour,
the glowing moon
always looks the same,
here and anywhere
I've ever been.

Some days I wonder,

How long will this go on?
How long can I go on?

I step back and listen,
straining my ears to hear
the familiar tom-tom
of my heartbeat drum
calling me forth
into another day.

Too often
I get the funny feeling
I'm not asking myself
the right questions.

Dear God,

What are
the right questions?

Other Voices

I never learn anything talking.
I only learn things when I ask questions.
~ Lou Holtz

January 22

IN EXILE
...we come to know our home.

So here I am,
back at home,
the very place
I always wanted to be,
the very place
I was afraid to remain,
because it was too small,
too traditional,
too cold and too hot,
too not the place to be
to change this world.

There's much truth
in everything I've said
about my hometown,
but I can only say it myself
because I packed my bags
and went where opportunity
paved an easy road.

Along my journey
I've come to understand
an even greater truth:

The most important change
I can most easily achieve
is within myself.

Other Voices

I know how men in exile feed on dreams.
~ AESCHYLUS

January 23

AFTER THE CURTAIN
...what will you do?

Do you stumble
into the New Year
like a runner falling
across the finish line?

Or do you burst forth,
shooting out of the gate
like a thoroughbred
at Churchill Downs?

Every year ends
with new beginnings,
but also begins
with old endings.

For some it's a time
to organize and reorder,
and maybe do something novel.

For others it's a time
to downsize and liquidate,
and maybe let go completely.

Other Voices

*Write it on your heart that every day
is the best day in the year.*
   ~ Ralph Waldo Emerson

January 24

IT'S ALL RIGHT
See for yourself.

Everything is all right.
Everything will be all right.
There is nothing I can say,
nothing I can do,
to make this more or less true.

In the past it felt
like an incredible burden
to be a part of God's creation,
while bearing humble witness
to the mysterious workings
of a seemingly random world
complicated by my free will.

Now I can no longer tell
if more and more of this life
is being wrested from my control,
or if I'm letting it go voluntarily,
shaking my head and laughing
because when I open my fists
there's nothing in them at all.

Other Voices

I know the sag of the unfinished poem.
And I know the release of the poem that is finished.
  ~ MARY OLIVER

January 25

THE HEART OF THE MATTER
...is often existential.

There's always a word or two
spoken by the voice in my head
that can summon an idea
right at the heart of the matter,
thus causing me to start listening.

Today the voice
grabbed my attention by asking,

What is it you fear?

I paused
before responding timidly,

Suffering.
I don't want to suffer.
. . .

Then,
as I let go of my focus,
in the distance I heard Jesus
calling out to Lazarus,

Come forth!
Come forth!

And so he did.

Other Voices

When you take your attention into the present moment, a certain alertness arises. You become more conscious of what's around you, but also, strangely, a sense of presence that is both within and without.
~ Eckhart Tolle

January 26

RIGHT NOW
...is where I want my focus.

When I truly relax
I'm able to recall yesterday
with a little more perspective,
as if I'm reading the news.

Yesterday's story begins
with a long and hot drive
through sweltering humidity
to join in my nephew's party.
And while I'm there resisting
risking my neck in the bouncy-house,
eating cupcakes with blue icing,
and drinking too much bourbon beer
while bullshitting with the big boys,
until the evening came to rescue me
with some much-needed calm
right before bed.

All in all it was a good time,
one of the many thousands
I've been lucky to have,
and must now try to let go
to make room for more.

Today I need
all of the space available
within my head and my heart
for what's happening right now.

Other Voices

*You can't depend on your eyes
when your imagination is out of focus.*
~ Mark Twain

January 27

THE MARKET MINDSET
...undermines everything.

So there you are, sitting
alone in a chain coffee shop,
bored by the same old apps
you've started neglecting
on your costly smartphone,
when out of thin air
a big idea comes to mind.

Your first instinct is to find a lawyer
who will protect your idea with patents
and introduce you to venture capitalists
who will ensure you find a market.

The plan works!
You make millions,
perhaps even billions.
Pundits call you a genius
(even though you repeated
second grade twice).

People,
houses, cars, jets,
power and private islands
- you purchase them all
to reinforce your myth.

But gosh darn it,
you're still bored!

No one warned you
a privileged life would be
too small and too unfulfilling,
too much everything you pined
to escape in the first place.

So now you pivot,
borrow more money
for a brand new company
that will build rocket ships
to send tourists into space.

All the while you're doubting,
yet still hopeful a new frontier
will give you needed perspective,
along with the coveted peace of mind
seemingly within your grasp,
but forever just out of reach.

*If outer space doesn't work,
then what's next?*

Other Voices

*The entrepreneur always searches for change,
responds to it, and exploits it as an opportunity.*
~ Peter Drucker

January 28

THE FIRST LINE
...will show you the way.

Trust the first line
spilling out of your mind
and onto the page.

Trust first
the very first word,
even if it
is nothing more
than a pause
to catch your breath,
or a pointer
directing attention
to what comes next.

The mind is a cannibal
and will eat you alive,
but it can't swallow the heart.
So lead with your heart.

Put your fingers on the paper.
Scratch the surface with your nail
to get a sense of the texture.

Next tap-tap your pen
until dots of ink appear
as you take dictation
from your soul.

Other Voices

*Faith is taking the first step
even when you don't see the whole staircase.*
~ Martin Luther King, Jr.

January 29

SERENITY SALESMEN
...sell sanctuary.

I'm a lousy salesman.
I sell serenity
but haven't closed a sale
to a single soul.

Maybe the price is too great.
Billionaires can't buy it.
You pay for it with blood
lost during the daily trials
of an honest life.

But just bleeding isn't enough.
You've got to weep for your losses,
and in night after endless night,
sleeplessly sweat out your anger.

Have I sold you yet?

Don't pay any attention to the way
my needless worry has aged me.

Serenity doesn't require
a young body,
the right job,
the right house,
the right spouse,
the right anything.

All that I can offer you
is my personal testimony.

Other Voices

*Despair is the damp of hell,
as joy is the serenity of heaven.*
~ JOHN DONNE

January 30

DON'T MAKE IT WORSE
Write this down.

Don't make it worse Brian,
says my superego.
I know you have the words
that can turn the knife inside him
making it sting all the more.

Say nothing and be silent.
Better yet, turn the other cheek.
Allow the fire to inflame your insides
burning out all of your anger.

Hasn't life taught you
victory is a lonely feeling
and falls like an acid rain,
destroying all the blooms
on our relationships?

In a world convinced of absolutes
perfection seems within your reach,
but please trust me when I tell you
life is already so much better
when you don't make it worse.

Other Voices

*Never stir up litigation.
A worse man can scarcely be found
than one who does this.*
~ ABRAHAM LINCOLN

January 31

DONNY FOOTBALL
May he rest in peace.

Another Don has died.
The first one, a close friend,
passed away in the summer
more than ten years ago.

This Don was an old friend's uncle,
a man I've known thirty five years.

Don was the quiet sort
with straight black hair,
always neatly parted.

Don suffered his life bravely,
smoked Winston Reds,
drank Miller High Life,
watched a lot of football,
and on occasion would say
the funniest things.

To be sure I knew Don
like a sailor knows an iceberg.
I am sharing with you what I saw,
but I didn't know the man beneath.

I'm told Don was a great athlete.
He was once married with kids.
He loved his family and friends.
Early on, he went off to Vietnam
where a part of him still remains.

If I gave this poem to Don
he probably wouldn't read it.
He often bragged
he'd read only one book:
Kon-Tiki.

Other Voices

*I also believe that when one dies,
one may wake up to the reality
that proves that time does not exist.*
  ~ Thor Heyerdahl

FEBRUARY

February 1

THE INVITATION
...may already be in your pocket.

Have you noticed a strange knocking,
but there's no one at the door?

Maybe you heard someone calling
your name out in a crowd.
And yet when you turned to look,
all you saw were strangers.

Perhaps once or twice today
you glanced down at your phone
to see several missed calls.

I wouldn't worry about it.
You're not losing your mind.
Someone or something
is trying to reach you.

Sooner or later that invitation
will find its way to you,
slipped beneath the door,
or left in a voicemail.

Yes, the invitation will come,
and though you may wish to refuse it,
your only real option will be to add it
to the others already in your pocket.

Then on the day you're ready,
you'll read one of those invitations
as you pass through a new doorway
and out into your spiritual journey.

Other Voices

A real conversation always contains an invitation.
~ David Whyte

February 2

THE ONLY WAY TO GET THERE
...is to go there.

I'm embarrassed
to acknowledge and to admit
to my own suffering.

I'm also often unaware
and subconsciously wanting
to deny my pain.

Why even bother
with something that's
too soft and sad,
mostly indescribable,
without reason,
self-inflicted,
unresolved
and unfixable?

But now I can see
those spirits who come
calling and urging me
to lean into my pain,
to feel and to understand
its depth and nuances.

I'm told there's
another side to this pain,
that given the opportunity
it may become a sacred wound
capable of great healing.

But the only way to get there
is to go through it.

Other Voices

*How can I sell sorrow,
when you know it's a blessing?*
~ RUMI

February 3

WITH ARMS WIDE
...to embrace your life

I tell myself,
think rhyme not reason.
Sing songs
using soulful words.
Accept the past,
and with arms wide open,
embrace the life you are given.

When I sit,
it's the stillness
expanding in the present
that reminds me serenity
exists within every atom,
emerging by invitation
or happy circumstance.

The child in me
never imagined this world
to be so troubled
that a good night's sleep
would not unleash
the healing power of serenity
all across the Universe.

Other Voices

*Love... it surrounds every being
and extends slowly to embrace all that shall be.*
~ KHALIL GIBRAN

February 4

WITHIN HIMSELF
...there is great love.

> Let me begin with a prayer
> for someone or something
> to come remind me
> nothing is wasted.
>
> I cannot calculate
> the vast amounts of time
> I silently stewed,
> thinking about everything
> I could be doing,
> or really should be doing.
>
> But now more often
> I look all around
> at this crazy-busy world
> and lament the years
> I spent lost in traffic,
> driving along endless roads,
> seeking things I couldn't see
> because they are so near.
>
> *Hear me!*
>
> Hear the prayer
> of a foolish man
> who got lost seeking
> love in externalities,
> but who now believes it's a waste
> to do anything other
> than to reveal the love
> within himself.

Other Voices

> *God's finger touched him,
> and he slept.*
> ~ Alfred Lord Tennyson

February 5

UNDERSTANDING AVENUE
...leads you further into unknowing.

Oh, how quickly
I can forget
the bitter truth
contained in the pain
I'd love to deny.

Each and every day
I make my way down
that long and winding road
called Understanding Avenue,
only to be led further,
and still further, away
from the absolute answers
I've so long desired.

For me peace comes
deep within the wilderness,
where it's easy to release
my desire to comprehend,
and easier to encounter God
in my unknowing.

Other Voices

*The clearest way into the Universe
is through a forest wilderness.*
~ JOHN MUIR

February 6

GO DEEP
...to find within you the stillness.

I feel like a wave
being pushed forward
by an invisible hand,
my swelling resistance
adding to the momentum
as I slowly rise and curl,
then crash headlong
back into myself.

Wave after wave
grows from within,
compelling me
into certain collision
with everything
water touches.

I am so tired
of the back and forth,
of the slow building
and the sudden ebbing
of my precious energy.

I just want to go deep
and lie low in the stillness.

Other Voices

Sit in reverie and watch the changing color of the waves that break upon the idle seashore of the mind.
~ HENRY WADSWORTH LONGFELLOW

February 7

A HEALING LIGHT
...comes from within.

What is it
repeatedly calling?
Calling me home,
back to my body,
back into my life
each and every
morning?

Could it be
I've yet to let go,
that there remains
so much more
for me to do?

A kindred spirit
comes to coax me,
insisting I examine
my aging scars.

Thus I begin noticing
a glowing light within,
the very same light I long
to share with others.

Other Voices

*Healing yourself
is connected with healing others.*
~ Yoko Ono

February 8

A PLACE TO ALWAYS
...rest in peace.

My old neighborhood
was built on abundant land,
just north of the great river
beside a spring-filled grove.

It must have been pretty then.
It must have been a sight to see.
I can picture the sycamore trees
standing amidst the rolling hills.

As a child I often wondered
where they found the heavy stones
to build the thick cemetery walls.
And I would watch the diesel trains,
forever coming and going,
clueless where the tracks led.

A hundred and fifty years ago
that creek and the railroad
must have meant a life and a living,
while the cemetery was perhaps
a place to always rest in peace.

Other Voices

*It may be that the satisfaction I need
depends on my going away,
so that when I've gone and come back,
I'll find it at home.*
  ~ Rumi

February 9

BEFORE BED
...I'll need a few things.

I need a good melody
to loosen my bones
and liberate my soul.

I need inspired lyrics
to remind me sweetly
of what I already know.

And I need to let go
as I dance a hundred dances,
collapsing into a deep sleep.

Then in the morning
I'll need to trip the light,
so upon waking I can see
what the new day has in store.

Other Voices

*If music be the food of love,
play on.*
~ WILLIAM SHAKESPEARE

February 10

REVISITING THE FLOW
...from whence we came...

Forget about the past.
Forget making things better.
Forget your pesky worries.
Forget that you once knew
all of the easy answers
to the toughest questions.

Now's the right time
to simply let it all go.

Now's the right time
to return to the flow.

Other Voices

Our birth is but a sleep and a forgetting;
The Soul that rises with us, our life's Star,
Hath had elsewhere its setting
And cometh from afar;
Not in entire forgetfulness,
And not in utter nakedness,
But trailing clouds of glory do we come
From God, who is our home:
Heaven lies about us in our infancy!
  ~ William Wordsworth

February 11

HOW SILLY
...I am.

How silly
all will one day seem:
our beliefs and mottoes,
our clichés and customs,
our laws and traditions.

In the long run
none of these can hold
even as much water
as an open hand.

And already none of them
can deliver us through
to another lifetime.

So I keep edging
ever closer to the fire,
allowing it singe my hair,
reminding me to live peacefully
on the red hot edges
of my true being.

Other Voices

*Do the best you can,
and don't take life too serious.*
~ WILL ROGERS

February 12

BIT O' GOLD
Let's call it a conversation.

There's a bit o' gold
in these and other words
I share with you.

Let's call it a conversation,
but maybe just between us,
and perhaps anyone else
who might stumble along.

Long before anyone cared
enough to write it down,
everyone and everything
engaged in dialogue.

And though many of us
converse to remember,
some do so to forget.
While others spend life
much too distracted
to say anything at all.

Believe it or not,
I also like to listen.
Outer space is silent.
Earth is a noisy place.

Other Voices

It was impossible to get a conversation going, everybody was talking too much.
~ Yogi Berra

February 13

SING ALONG
...and become a poet.

Silver space pen,
purple notebook,
brown blanket,
yellow dog,
blue morning,
black tea...

Inside my head
I'm humming soul music,
dark notes of longing,
bright words of belonging.

Love is
green, orange, red,
and the chorus goes:

*Sing, sing,
sing for some bread.
Sing, sing,
sing and be fed.*

With calming notes
I summon my muse,
then light a candle
to scribble out
my song.

Other Voices

*Every heart sings a song, incomplete,
until another heart whispers back.
Those who wish to sing always find a song.
At the touch of a lover, everyone becomes a poet.*
~ PLATO

February 14

BE PATIENT
...fire will find you.

It's so hard to sit
and become still
when you're young
and full of that stuff
that pushes the trees
up toward the heavens,
that moves the mountains
along their rolling trajectory,
that sends a bird instinctively
on a journey thousands of miles long.

Do whatever you must do
to garner life experience
and the wisdom it offers.
But remember also to listen
to the irritating old women
who still love you dearly
despite seeing your kind
countless times before.

Heed them when they warn:

Don't go lookin' for fire.
Fire will find you.

Other Voices

Who ever is out of patience
is out of possession of their soul.
~ Francis Bacon

February 15

HOW TO FORGET
...is an art.

There's an art to forgetting
so that the forgotten
never returns.

Some forgetting is only
a suspension of remembering,
allowing us time to reconsider
other aspects of the forgotten.

Some remembering is only
the stubborn refusal
to release our past
into oblivion.

Some forgetting is innocent.
Some remembering is inevitable.

Some of us will master
the art of forgetting,
while others will prefer
to remember forever.

Other Voices

How happy is the blameless vestal's lot!
The world forgetting, by the world forgot.
Eternal sunshine of the spotless mind!
Each pray'r accepted, and each wish resign'd?
~ ALEXANDER POPE

February 16

THE SILENT SONGS
…we're all singing.

Surely there are silent songs
sung everywhere simultaneously,
on Sundays and Wednesdays,
on Tuesdays and Saturdays,
by sopranos and tenors,
on empty sidewalks,
in suburban forests,
in the cars stalled
on crowded super highways.

Surely there's a silent song
in a story that makes us sad,
in a kiss of sweet chocolate,
or in a silly little poem
seeming to suggest
the whole world is singing
from the same song book:

Being.

Other Voices

I don't sing because I'm happy;
I'm happy because I sing.
~ WILLIAM JAMES

February 17

CALENDAR APP
Have you got one?

Oh hello Wednesday!
It's not bad for a Monday.
I can't remember last Thursday.
Wait, when's the par-tay?

The calendar app may be
the best tool I ever bought.
I use it more and more
the busier my life gets.
My loyalty is rewarded
with timely reminders
and spot on directions.

The calendar app tells me
where I've been,
where I'm going,
how busy I've become,
and maybe, just maybe,
to a marketer perhaps,
who I really am.

Keeping a calendar
keeps me out of trouble.
But by far my favorite days
are still the empty ones.

Other Voices

*The time you enjoy wasting
is not wasted time.*
~ BERTRAND RUSSELL

February 18

IT'S IN THE MIDDLES
...where we all must live.

Take the superlatives.
You can have them.
I don't want 'em,
don't need 'em here
where I'm living
in-between.

I hope for the best,
often fear the worst,
yet would much rather
compromise for the good,
or even the not-so-bad.

Would that I could so easily
let go of my life preserver
and calmly float upon
life's endless waves,
from top to bottom
and back up again.

Other Voices

*It is in middles that extremes clash,
where ambiguity restlessly rules.*
~ JOHN UPDIKE

February 19

RECLAMATION
Re-purpose your loyal soldiers.

It's time to let go
of everything not working
in sympathy and solidarity
with your renewed efforts
to exhume your precious soul
from that resting place
where you buried it long ago
promising never to return.

Gather your loyal soldiers,
those who once helped you
to prepare the shallow grave,
then ushered your body off
for last rites.

Be sure to thank them
for their devoted service
in all the survival battles
you waged together.

But let them know
the war is finally over
and the time has come
for you to reclaim your soul
in everlasting peace.

Other Voices

Every lover serves as a soldier, also Cupid has his own camp;
Believe me, Atticus, every lover serves as a soldier.
  ~ Ovid

February 20

LIFE DEMANDS
...something called unknowing.

Once you see something,
you'll always see it.
It's much the same
with the other senses.

What you hear and smell,
both taste and touch,
becomes part of you,
a permanent knowing.

This must be why we resist
when life demands from us
something called unknowing

At some point we must unsee
and look again with new eyes.

We must stop tuning in
to those same old voices
and listen to someone new.

We must allow our feelings to pass
and experience true emptiness.

There's no doubt
I could say it much better,
if only I'd let go
of the same old words.

Other Voices

*The only thing worse than being blind
is having sight but no vision.*
~ Helen Keller

February 21

FOREVER
...as seen through the prism of nostalgia.

Where did it all go,

that rock you found,
the endless summer,
grandma's pumpkin pie,
high school and college,
radio and records,
black and white images,
the Tooth Fairy,
Saturday cartoons,
staticky screens,
Wite-Out,
ashtrays,
sidewalks,
loitering Vietnam Vets,
pop bottles,
yo-yos,
Now and Laters,
Closed signs,
nothing to do
but sit and watch
the day go by?

What happened
to not worrying at all,
convinced life
would go on like this
forever?

Other Voices

Nostalgia is a file that removes the rough edges from the good old days.
~ Doug Larson

February 22

NEW MEANING
...can be found in old melodies.

Sometimes an old melody
will come back to bite me,
bringing with it lyrics
I seem to be hearing
for the very first time.

The familiar tune
doesn't bother knocking,
just comes right in,
sits in front of me and says,
"Listen again."

This time the words
shoot through me like electricity,
traveling along all the vines
which have grown out of my heart
over the past twenty years.

My soul is an unkempt garden
wanting me to grow wild
by experiencing my life again,
this time more aware
of who I truly am.

Other Voices

*I'm saying: to be continued, until we meet again.
Meanwhile, keep on listening and tapping your feet.*
~ COUNT BASIE

February 23

BLEEDING
...dripping, blending, combining...

Some evenings
end too late.
Some mornings
begin too early.

Everything
bleeds
into every
other thing.

The wind picks up,
blowing water and dust
around the globe
in all directions.

The puddles overflow,
spilling into creeks,
forming rivers,
feeding the oceans.

Some things sit
a thousand years
resisting the wind
and the rain.

I'm up too early,
gone to bed too late,
spread too thinly
across time and space.

Other Voices

*I believe in running through the rain
and crashing into the person you love
and having your lips bleed on each other.*
  ~ Billy Bob Thornton

February 24

ACCEPT THE CALL
...to consciousness.

I can't tell
whether my life
is getting easier
or becoming harder,
as I go along.

The clean-shaven wise guy
looking back in the mirror
smirks and chides me,
"Play the game, man!"

But I've come too far,
glimpsed enough truth
behind all the lies
and no longer have time
for childish games.

Music calms me,
picks the locks protecting
my big ole heavy heart,
sprays perfume in the air,
and then gets me drunk
just so I'll dance.

A whiny voice crackles
over an old speaker,
"When ya ain't got nothin',
you got nothin' to lose."

Except I've got things
keeping me up at night,
'cause I'm frightened
I might lose 'em.

The old hippie doctor
says on his podcast,
"Take ten deep breaths.
Now how do you feel?"

I feel light-headed,
but see what he means.
The only real difference
between war and peace,
is a simple choice.

Life does get easier
even as it becomes harder,
by accepting who I am
and what I must do.

Other Voices

Happiness can exist only in acceptance.
  ~ GEORGE ORWELL

February 25

ALL GOES AWAY
...

There's nothing profound
I can think of to say,
other than it's true
all will one day go away.

This place,
those people,
that church and steeple,
the rock over there,
my favorite easy chair,
you and me,
him, her, them, we
will all someday
go away.

Even things said
to last forever
will eventually succumb
to time and the weather.

Maybe you like
this status quo,
but I truly thought
you'd like to know.

I heartily suggest
you go out and play
before the time
this all goes away.

Other Voices

It is the end. But of what?
The end of France? No.
The end of kings? Yes.
~ Victor Hugo

February 26

IN THE DIRT
...is where you are rooted.

Don't be fooled
by the stars
twinkling in the sky.

Pay little attention
to the birds
soaring overhead.

Staring at the rising
and the setting sun
won't reveal the meaning
of your precious life.

For that
don't look up,
you look down.

Let your eyes fall
past your knees,
beneath your toes
to the ground below.

Up is a distraction.
It's too big for you to know
and will leave you despairing
of its emptiness.

Down in the dirt
is where you are rooted,
in the thick mud and muck
of all being.

Other Voices

A human being has so many skins inside, covering the depths of the heart. We know so many things, but we don't know ourselves! Why, thirty or forty skins or hides, as thick and hard as an ox's or bear's, cover the soul. Go into your own ground and learn to know yourself there.
    ~ Meister Eckhart

February 27

NOW I KNOW
...pretty much who I am.

Next week
it'll be Thursday again,
and though I may not be
exactly the same then,
I'll bet I'm close to it.

It's taken a few years,
but at last I've come to know
pretty much who I am.

More and more often,
I find myself letting go
of who I thought I was
or one day have to become.

This past Monday
I think I heard my soul
out singing in the rain.

Now that's new.

Other Voices

*Knowing others is wisdom,
knowing yourself is Enlightenment.*
~ Laozi

February 28

RIVER WISDOM
...flows within us.

I go to River
and River says,
Come closer,
I know you.

I say,
Great River,
I have been here before.

River responds,
I am the same water
flowing through your veins.
But don't try to tame me
as your world has tamed you.

I ask River,
How can I cross
to your other side?

River says,
Don't try to swim me,
you'll be pulled under.
And don't take all my water,
I'll just go underground.
Ask your soul to build a boat,
then gently go with my flow.

Other Voices

The river flows at its own sweet will,
but the flood is bound in the two banks.
If it were not thus bound,
its freedom would be wasted.
~ Vinoba Bhave

February 29

RIVER RETURN
There's always more wisdom.

Again I go back,
treading more lightly,
seeking further wisdom
from the slow-moving river.

Stand back,
says River.

Wherever I flow,
I make the ground muddy.
My currents are treacherous
and may pull you under.

I pause to ponder
River's stern warning,
marveling at the mighty flow
passing right before me.

River senses my hesitation
and speaks again, more softly.

You have not cried enough.
When you are ready
return, bringing along
your salty tears.

I will carry them
to the sea.

Other Voices

Religion and ritual can be vehicles for entering stillness. It says in Psalm 46:10, 'Be still, and know that I am God.' But they are still just vehicles. The Buddha called his teaching a raft: You don't need to carry it around with you after you've crossed the river.
~ Eckhart Tolle

MARCH

March 1

QUANTUM MECHANICS
...is where entropy becomes serendipity.

A physicist can tear a hole
in my happy knowing
more easily than I can
tear a piece of paper.

Seeing the world through
a prism of quantum mechanics
untethers my very being
from this time and place,
catapulting me through
the vacuum of infinite space.

I feel dizzy,
staggered on my feet,
worried because one atom,
one electron or random photon,
may be all the difference
between me living out my life,
or spinning into oblivion.

Other Voices

If quantum mechanics hasn't profoundly shocked you, you haven't understood it yet.
~ Niels Bohr

March 2

A TIME TO REST
...my traveling soul.

It's half-past five when
the wheels touch down.
After six hours in the air
I'm so glad to be home.

First things first,
so I pull off the highway
looking for a place to eat.

That's when I notice
the awesome pink sunset
and an eerie stillness.

While far away I forgot
winter is now upon us,
and this place I call home
now welcomes me quietly,
with an invitation to rest
my traveling soul.

Other Voices

*In seed time learn,
in harvest teach,
in winter enjoy.*
— WILLIAM BLAKE

March 3

THE WALLS
...always do fall.

For too many
our infinite world
is encircled by walls.

And yet light still
can sometimes penetrate
the porous constructs
of human certitude.

There are those standing
outside the walls.

There are those digging
beneath the walls.

There are those on guard
atop the walls.

There are those waiting
for the walls to fall.

And the walls
always do fall.

Other Voices

Love recognizes no barriers.
It jumps hurdles, leaps fences, penetrates walls
to arrive at its destination full of hope.
   ~ Maya Angelou

March 4

THERE'S STILL TIME
...and lots of it.

There's still time,
no matter what
the clock says.

There's always another day,
a second or third chance,
a free forty-five minutes.

There's still time,
no matter what
the barometer says.

There'll be rain tomorrow
with lots of wind and cold,
but sun the following day.

There's still time,
no matter what
the pundits think.

We've got much to do,
with plenty of loose ends,
but also plenty of help.

And there's still time
no matter what
the mirror shows you.

Don't be concerned.
Everyone knows
mirrors lie.

Other Voices

*You don't always have to be doing something.
You can just be, and that's plenty.*
~ Alice Walker

March 5

I AM OVERCOME
...by the silence.

What must be said
is often unwritten
and rarely spoken.

Therefore we must live
from inside the inevitable truth,
which begins at our birth
and accelerates throughout
our difficult initiations.
From lust and desire,
through feast and famine;
from loss and death,
through long periods
of bitterness and despair,
preceding our return
to innocence.

We must find the sources
of those stories and songs,
which halt and disarm,
rendering us speechless.

There in the deafening silence
we encounter God.

Other Voices

*After silence,
that which comes nearest
to expressing the inexpressible
is music.*
   ~ Aldous Huxley

March 6

THE VEIL LIFTED
...for a brief moment.

For a brief moment
I noticed the veil lifting
and saw spirits approaching
with gifts to share.

But I reacted too fiercely
and frightened them away.

The veil has now fallen,
and I can no longer hear
their whispering voices
or see their shadows.

I said nothing,
but my heart leapt out,
desperate and rapacious,
calling out wildly:

*Tell me what to do
with the rest of my life!*

Other Voices

*Death is the veil which those who live call life;
They sleep, and it is lifted.*
~ Percy Bysshe Shelley

March 7

IMPƏRFƏCT LOVƏ
...is all there is.

That imperfect love
you've been cursing,
desperately clinging to,
silently resenting,
returning conditionally
while hoarding it
before spilling some out
like cheap beer in a tavern,
only later to chop it up
for sale to the highest bidder,
except that piece you're saving
for a special someone...

Yes,
that imperfect love,
your imperfect love,
along with mine,
and hers, his,
their imperfect love -
gather it all up.

Pour it all over yourself.
Pour it all over everyone
and all over everything
you encounter.

This Universe
desperately wants
all of our offerings
of imperfect love.

Other Voices

*It belongs to the imperfection of everything human
that man can only attain his desire
by passing through its opposite.*
 ~ SØREN KIERKEGAARD

March 8

GROWING SPACE
...is as essential as fresh air.

When the space
where you now reside
starts to feel like a prison,
your soul will likely begin
asking for more room.

Growing may not be easy,
but it's better than the blowback
of an angry and confined soul
unable to fully express itself.

Other Voices

*If you surrendered to the air,
you could ride it.*
~ Tony Morrison

March 9

MY PLANS
...are just a rough draft.

Less than an hour
after my waking,
I crumbled up
my plans for today.
I quickly threw them
into the white hot flame
I once called resentment,
though it seems to burn
brighter and warmer now
since I renamed it
my acceptance.

I thank God along with
those mischievous spirits,
for keeping me off-balance
and without a firm agenda.

Their intervention saved me
from myself and from spending
all day in the insanely tiny cell
I constructed for my soul.

Other Voices

*If you want to make God laugh,
tell him about your plans.*
~ WOODY ALLEN

March 10

WISE COUNSEL
...is abetted by necessity.

In the cold too bitter
and the wind too fierce,
I watched the first half
feeling a bit dejected.

I stood there frozen,
like a marionette tethered
to a barbaric puppet master
whose outdated and macho ideas
of what it means to be a real fan
had superseded any common sense.

At halftime I proposed
we seek out a warmer place
to view the second half,
and perhaps better enjoy
a hard-fought victory.

My friend blinked in disbelief,
then slowly began to absorb
the once heretical notion
of ever leaving a game early.

In fact, he now found leaving
quite agreeable after wise counsel
from his frozen toes.

Other Voices

Search well and be wise,
nor believe that self-willed pride
will ever be better than good counsel.
— AESCHYLUS

March 11

TRUTH
...frees the bound soul.

Truth is truth
regardless of how it enters
the bloodstream.

When told they're loved,
even those who struggle
to tell the truth,
quite easily stumble into
a divine authenticity.

We all know truth,
from its universality
all the way through
to its genuine devotion.

Truth is a big relief,
much like being reminded:
*If you can understand it,
then it is not God.*

Truth is freedom
from having to know,
and also the freedom
from wasting any time
listening to those
who think they do.

Other Voices

*It's no wonder that truth is stranger than fiction.
Fiction has to make sense.*
~ MARK TWAIN

March 12

MY SCREENS
...are portals into darkness.

Three empty screens
are staring back at me.

The matte black face
shows me nothing,
but the glossy ones
are like dark mirrors
reflecting the shadows
inside my tiny office.

These three screens
are attached to a world
much bigger and darker
than I can imagine.

When I turn them on
they glow dazzlingly,
concealing the secrets
of where they've been
with colorful images
and bouncing icons.

I cover the tiny cameras
atop these empty screens,
not wanting the darkness
to see into my soul.

Other Voices

Deep into that darkness peering, long I stood there, wondering,
Fearing, doubting, dreaming dreams no mortal
ever dared to dream before...
    ~ Edgar Allen Poe

March 13

HOW I LOVE
...now that I know...

As my love grows,
my long list
of likes and dislikes
is shrinking.

I now love the rain.
I love the snow.
Above all I love
those spirits helping
the flowers to grow.

I love the desert.
I love the sea.
I love the vines
growing wildly between
you and me.

I love my suffering.
I love my joy.
I love my life.
I know there's nothing
I need to destroy.

I love you.
I love me.
I love this world.
Oh, how I love all three!

Other Voices

That is the real spiritual awakening, when something emerges from within you that is deeper than who you thought you were. So, the person is still there, but one could almost say that something more powerful shines through the person.
  ~ Eckhart Tolle

March 14

SLOW DANCING
...requires music and time.

I call to those spirits
who like to move slowly,
like an earthworm.

I ask them to pour
their mystical sand
into the human gears
grinding and whirling,
driving everyone crazy
at ever faster speeds
towards something
akin to death.

Yes, I need time away
from industrious activity
to recharge and reorient
the wayward spirit within.
My soul wants community
but this world we're creating
is displacing all of us into
silos of individuality.

I remember those signs
reading *Closed Sundays*,
and waiting and watching
for the trains to pass.

Do you remember
the winter weather
keeping you inside,
with nowhere to go
and nothing to do?

Do your remember
having a big question
and not being able to find
a quick or easy answer?

Other Voices

*If you do not change direction,
you may end up where you are heading.*
    ~ Laozi

March 15

LIFE IS FINE
...may be a barefaced lie.

I just read a poem
written by a young man
living at a Harlem YMCA
while studying English.

He's come from the South,
but has traveled even further,
transcending time and place
to tell me his story.

It's not too unusual,
or even too improbable,
but it's a black man's story
written nearly a century ago.

And it's not a story
that everyone knows,
unless they understand it
from personal experience.

Not a tale
we all want to hear,
it asks us to grapple
with our own stories,
to consider, perhaps,
how our happy ignorance
makes us utterly complicit
in the face of great evil.

Other Voices

I went down to the river,
I set down on the bank.
I tried to think but couldn't
So I jumped in and sank.

I came up once and hollered!
I came up twice and cried!
If that water hadn't a-been so cold
I might've sunk and died...
    ~ Langston Hughes

March 16

DO SOMETHING
...that really matters.

The sign in their yard
says *Do Something*
in bold red letters against
a black background.

It seems rather angry,
so I don't plan asking
what it means,
or who it's referring to.

All the same,
I know the sentiment.
There's not enough stuff
getting done that's needing done.
And there's too much doing
of utter nonsense.

It complicates matters
that some of us probably
ought to be doing less,
while allowing others
a chance to do more.

Other Voices

*Life's most persistent and urgent question is,
What are you doing for others?*
~ Martin Luther King, Jr.

March 17

GO OUT AND PLAY
(you know you want to)

There's much to do,
yet so little demanding
to be done.

Most work
is just busy work,
the Christian way
of keeping demons
safely at bay.

Try to think more slowly,
and of all those things
you can easily let go.

Ask your soul
what to do today,
and it will likely say,
Go out and play!

Other Voices

*Idle hands are the devil's workshop;
idle lips are his mouthpiece.*
~ Proverbs 16:27

March 18

TINY ARROWS
...like rays of light

All lights,
even the dim ones,
may be asking you
to see something.

Light is illumination
in an otherwise
dark world.

I see what I see.
You see what you see.

But don't we both see
the billions of tiny arrows
pointing every which way
toward God?

Other Voices

*Nature makes only dumb animals.
We owe the fools to society.*
~ Honoré de Balzac

March 19

THE BLUE PILL
...of forgetfulness

I'm lookin'
and she's lookin',
you're lookin',
and he's lookin',
all of us are lookin'
for some way out
of the straitjacket
confining us to a life
of financial slavery,
while lookin' for a way off
this bullet train to oblivion,
and lookin' for a way into
meaningful relationship
with Mother Earth,
with Father Time,
with Sister Moon,
and Brother Sun.

We're lookin'
for something real,
something we can hold,
something sweet and sour,
beyond any consciousness,
only glimpsed in our dreams,
yet still awake in our souls,
which for way too long
have been buried alive -

since the day we swallowed
the blue pill of forgetfulness.

Other Voices

This is your last chance. After this there is no turning back. You take the blue pill, the story ends. You wake up in your bed and believe whatever you want to. You take the red pill, you stay in Wonderland, and I show you how deep the rabbit hole goes. Remember, all I'm offering is the truth. Nothing more.
~ Morpheus

March 20

MY OWN WORST ENEMY
I am.

I suppose others saw it
sooner than I ever could.
From a distance they whispered,
He's his own worst enemy.

These middle years are tough.
Life's disappointments mount.
There's now a ledger of losses,
which can never be reconciled.

And no matter how much
I try to hold on to,
there's always more escaping
out my back door.

I've worked hard,
tried to do things right.
I fought and I fixed,
but life kept coming
wave after wave.

I'm tired of resisting,
forever living the cliché,
running against the wind,
paddling upstream.

My prayer is simple.
I ask for a community
to share this burden
that I once truly thought
was mine alone to bear.

Other Voices

*Beware of no man more than of yourself;
we carry our worst enemies within us.*
~ Charles Spurgeon

March 21

CIRCLES
...concentric, overlapping...

These days I keep sayin'
there's nothing I must do.

And this of course is true.
Of all those things I believed
were required of me:

the learning,
the earning,
the spending,
the defending,
the climbing,
and the denying,

none of them were needed,
or even necessary.

As I learn my true place
and take my seat within
the unbroken circle of life,
I find a new list of things
that are mine to do:

letting go and loving,
steadily descending and bending
toward the humble ground,
singing, dancing, and celebrating
the beauty and the belonging
of everyone and everything.

Other Voices

*I don't believe that life is linear.
I think of it as circles -
concentric circles that connect.*
    ~ Michelle Williams

March 22

TENDERNESS
Let's try a little.

Try a little tenderness.
Everything is made more difficult
through resentment and resistance
and pushing back on anything
now pushing against you.

Through physics we learn
every action produces
an equal and opposite reaction.

Through relationships we learn
a yes is easily met with a no,
and big questions are never settled.

The solution is simple:
We must try a little tenderness,
and only offer resistance
when it's in everyone's best interest.

We can only expect tenderness
from those who experience tenderness.

Other Voices

Try a little tenderness
(That's all you gotta do)
~ Song Lyrics written by Jimmy Campbell,
Reg Connelly, and Harry M. Woods.

March 23

DON'T BUY MORE CLOTHES
...wear the ones you have.

I begin counting backwards
starting at one hundred,
and before getting to eighty
I'm fast asleep and being visited
by strangely familiar strangers
offering their wisdom in riddles.

Now that I'm awake, I refuse
to count myself back to that place
where the spirits can manipulate
my unguarded psyche.

So I wrestle to stay awake,
even though I know there's a space
between this world and that one
to make peace with ambiguity.

Other Voices

*I say,
beware of all enterprises that require new clothes,
and not rather a new wearer of clothes.*
~ Henry David Thoreau

March 24

BECOMING SPEECHLESS
...makes you a plaintiff.

I believe everyone here with us
has somehow stumbled
into a transcendent dimension
where nouns and adjectives
have lost their meanings,
and the only relevant terms
are *being* and *loving*.

You don't have to ask
someone to tell the story
about their journey through
the thin veil separating worlds.

They will offer it
to everyone and everything,
in their own time
and in their own ways.

You will one day believe the truth
inherent in their life experience,
when you see it beautifully manifest
in their simple, loving acts.

Being rendered speechless
will someday make you a plaintiff,
when you encounter others who fearfully deny
their own sublime encounters.

Other Voices

*In this day the breeze of God is wafted,
and His Spirit hath pervaded all things.
Such is the outpouring of His grace
that the pen is stilled
and the tongue is speechless.*
~ BAHÁ'U'LLÁH

March 25

HIS MOTHER
...imagined in a poem.

His mom died on Friday,
and of course there were tears.

He posted her picture on Facebook
along with a link to her obituary.
Many offered their condolences
in the comments section.

I left mine
in line with the others,
adding an emoji dove
and a beating heart.

He replied to me,
*My mom remembered poetry
from her childhood.*

I never met his mom,
but I can imagine her in a poem.

She's alive en el desierto,
at home near la frontera,
in una mezcla de culturas,
connected to este mundo
by una historia beyond
my limited comprensión.

May she rest in peace,
so her son may also
rest in peace.

Other Voices

Men are what their mothers made them.
~ Ralph Waldo Emerson

PRICKLY PEOPLE
...I know 'em so well.

Twice a year I give thanks
for all the prickly people in my life.
Some of them came into life that way,
and I guess others got unlucky.

But now here they all are,
one finger always poking at me
while they go about their business
in annoying detail or utter sloppiness.

I can never quite tell
if they're coming or going
because they clog the roads
and slow down our progress.

They ask stupid questions,
are ready to believe anyone,
and tragically seem to lack
the common sense of a potato.

They live on the coasts
and also in the mountains.
But I fear the majority dwell
right here in my neighborhood.

These prickly people are everywhere.
They went to the same schools as me,
cheer for the same teams as me,
and complain about the same things.

I know these prickly people so well
because I am one of them.

Other Voices

*You use a glass mirror to see your face;
you use works of art to see your soul.*
~ George Bernard Shaw

March 27

ONIONS
...are underappreciated.

Sure we like onions,
but few of us love them
like those lovers of garlic
or the chocoholics.

I summon the onion
to mind, heart and gut,
because there may be
no more perfect metaphor
for the spiritual life.

Day by day we peel away
the layers of our being.
Each layer is a bit smaller
and strangely more fragrant.

We may never reach the center.
But even if we could manage
there would be no great reward,
only more onion.

Other Voices

For an Apple is in itself a little Universe;
the Seed, hotter than the other parts thereof, is its Sun,
which diffuses about itself that natural Heat
which preserves its Globe: And in the Onion,
the Germ is the little Sun of that little World,
which vivifies and nourishes
the vegetative Salt of that little mass.
~ Cyrano de Bergerac

March 28

GIVING MYSELF
...to love unconditionally.

I fall in love so easily
with an idea,
a piece of music,
or an image
and a way
of seeing things.

Yet I struggle
to love my life
and the people in it.

It takes me a while
to fall for a friend,
a cute little baby,
or a better idea.

But I have a soul,
and so eventually
I am able to let go,
giving myself over
to unconditional love.

Other Voices

The ultimate lesson all of us have to learn is unconditional love, which includes not only others but ourselves as well.
~ Elisabeth Kübler-Ross

March 29

ACQUIESCENCE
...to my imperfection.

I am broken,
or at least cracked
and a little bit frayed
around the edges.

I hate being this way,
not able to fix myself,
not able to figure it out,
and not any different
from the imperfection
all around me.

I apologize,
aware I've written
this same poem
many times before.

And yet every time
I revisit my brokenness,
I inch just a bit closer
to some kind of acceptance.

Other Voices

*Existence really is an imperfect tense
that never becomes a present.*
~ Friedrich Nietzsche

March 30

IMMIGRANT SONG
An ode to empathy.

Let's go to the ocean.
Sand and shells in a bottle
don't tell the whole story.

I need to know why
staring at them on the shelf
brings wave upon wave
of cold, thirsty convulsion.

I don't know the ocean
as someone dwelling nearby
or toiling for a living upon it.

Yet I'm drawn to the water
as if the moon is seducing me
with her undulating passion.

Somehow, somewhere,
sometime long, long ago,
I crossed over that body,
only to now find myself
alive in this one.

Other Voices

*Your loving does not know its majesty
until it knows its helplessness.*
~ RUMI

March 31

TIME IS RELATIVE
...in measuring change and growth.

In a decade
a rock hardly moves,
but a child will grow
from infant to independent.

In a decade
the sun and the moon
endlessly exchange shifts
as they have for eons.

In a decade
all of my favorite songs
fade or change into anthems
of prayer and gratitude.

With each decade
time moves still faster,
as I slowly begin to realize
gold is flowing in my veins.

Other Voices

*Adjusting to the passage of time,
I think, is a key to success and to life:
just being able to roll with the punches.*
~ DOLLY PARTON

APRIL

April 1

JUST LET IT HAPPEN
Say yes.

What is the meaning of light?
And what is the value of yes?

No one really knows
until they've spent time
lost in the darkness,
unable to say yes.

How many noes equal a yes?
And how much time is wasted
building walls and monuments
in reverence to stubbornness?

Until yes becomes a reflex
and no is just something
lost in your drawer,
follow that man,
follow that woman,
who loves every song,
agrees with everyone,
and feels right at home
everywhere.

Other Voices

The big question is whether you are going
to be able to say a hearty yes to your adventure.
   ~ Joseph Campbell

April 2

A SEED
Indeed!

Don't whisper
when you say,
I love you.

Repetition
removes uncertainty,
so keep breathing
until you awaken
into the fullness
of your being.

That voice urging you
to do what's yours to do,
knows you are a seed.

Other Voices
*Your heart is full of fertile seeds,
waiting to sprout.*
~ Morihei Ueshiba

A GOOD SEAT
...at the table of life.

Make me a reservation
for a seat at the table;
buy me a ticket so I can tag along.

I want to go with.
For so long I've been without
and didn't even know it.

I once thought
I could do everything
on my own time,
and in my own way.

Now my time is too precious,
and so, too, is belonging.

Other Voices

*I had therefore to remove knowledge,
in order to make room for belief.*
~ IMMANUEL KANT

April 4

START LISTENING
...to your soul.

This is how you'll know
where to make room for change,
what you need to start drinking
to refresh your dry palate.

How easily you forget
what it means to be young,
what it means to be alive,
not existing and persisting
in defiance of time.

Your soul is seeking a revelation
and has been longing to grow
since your first sip of milk,
your first gulp of air.

*Listen to all the sounds
now ringing in your ears!*

What is there to do
if you refuse to wake up,
to show up and grow up,
to answer your life calling you
into communion with everything?

Other Voices

*To forget one's purpose
is the commonest form of stupidity.*
~ Friedrich Nietzsche

INUNDATED
...an ode in two parts...

Part 1

When I'm overwhelmed,
I notice my wife is bewildered
by the incomplete thoughts
spilling out of my mouth
in seemingly random phrases.

Often, it's just a song verse
triggered by something I heard,
or maybe it's my loyal soldier
trying to devise an escape
from this demanding moment.

Part 2

I tell you sincerely,
nothing is more seductive to me
than to be free of all responsibility.

But I know just as well,
commitment is my salvation,
even when it feels like a wet blanket.

I like being asked to help.
I like being asked to participate.
Yet sometimes just the asking
drowns me in a sea of yeses.

*So how does a drowning man
get back to shore and dry land?*

He follows the bubbles to the surface,
then allows the current to carry him.

Other Voices

*The individual has always had to struggle
to keep from being overwhelmed by the tribe.
If you try it, you will be lonely often,
and sometimes frightened.
But no price is too high to pay
for the privilege of owning yourself.*
    ~ Friedrich Nietzsche

April 6

PRAY CONSTANTLY
...as lovers do.

I'm not awake,
yet our conversation
continues here and now,
yanked from the dream world
into a space that feels
deceptively solid.

Rumi assures me,
Lovers pray constantly.

Now I no longer doubt
this is what I've been doing,
both night and day,
whether hot or cold,
mile after dusty mile,
my heart soaked in tears.

I want to move
like time moves,
sneakily,
silently,
only noticed
at the mile markers of life.

I thought I was dying,
but just maybe
I'm being born again.

Other Voices

We meet at this appointed time.
You've read where it says that
Lovers pray constantly.
Once a day, once a week, five times an hour,
Is not enough. Fish like we
Need the ocean around us.
Do camel-bells say, Let's meet again
Thursday night?
Ridiculous. They jingle
Together continuously,
Talking while the camel walks.
Do you pay regular visits to yourself?
Don't argue or answer rationally.
And dying, reply.
  ~ Rumi

April 7

RIGHT HERE, RIGHT NOW
...is the place to be.

I know, oh, I know
when I'm blocking the flow,
stifling the spirit,
holding up the show.

Here,
but really anywhere,
is the last place I want to be,
alone with my thoughts.

I used to just go
wherever wit and whim
would carry me,
but I never got very far
until I stopped moving.

The biggest questions
are all easily answered
with patience and presence,
right here, right now.

Other Voices

*Absence sharpens love,
presence strengthens it.*
~ Thomas Fuller

April 8

ICE AGE TRUTH
You knew it all along.

Try, try again,
is the age-old adage
now ringing in your ears.

What you're hearing
is the sound of the empty road,
wheels turning in your mind,
but your heart is hovering,
afraid the asphalt will deliver
an existential truth.

Down and in,
moving closer together,
that's what the day demands.

You've been chasing the horizon
since the ice last receded.
All the while the truth
has been gaining from behind.

When it bites you on your ass
you'll probably laugh, saying,
I knew it all along.

Other Voices

*Three things cannot be long hidden:
the sun, the moon, and the truth.*
~ BUDDHA

April 9

LIGHTEN YOUR LOAD
...by letting go of some memories.

Some people are just gonna
have to remind me of their names,
and my wife's just gonna
have to find some patience
when I forget movies we've seen.

There's simply too much
for me to remember it all now,
and I'm not really interested
in keeping everything straight.

There's the important stuff,
like the people I live with
and all those memories
which give my life context.

Everything else is more than
what's absolutely necessary
to make me a loving person
and help me through this day.

There's so much dead weight
sitting in my bag of memories.
Why not lighten the load a little
by letting go of the silly ones?

The needed memories will remain
as guiding spirits on the road ahead.

Other Voices

*The trick to forgetting the big picture
is to look at everything close-up.*
~ Chuck Palahniuk

April 10

ONCE YOU SEE
...it's hard to unsee.

Any drunk will tell us
they drink for reasons
we can all understand.

Most truths are bitter,
hard enough to swallow,
and harder to accept.

I must accept my life
will never be lived perfectly,
knowing I'll always struggle
not to judge others.

I find it so easy,
not taking illicit drugs
or drinking to excess.

Yet I struggle mightily
to suppress the rage I feel
at my own powerlessness
to change the way things are.

Other Voices

*We must let go of the life we have planned,
so as to accept the one that is waiting for us.*
    ~ Joseph Campbell

April 11

LIGHTNESS OF BEING
…is awaiting you now.

When I lapse into longing,
it's never for one thing,
a single moment in time.

No,
I long for large swaths
of undefinable time
and uncertain place,
always a little fuzzy,
but no less credible
than this heartfelt poem
of fond recollection.

I long for times
when I saw everything
with new eyes.

I long for times
every song soothed me
like a sweet lullaby.

I long for times
when each encounter held
mystery and magic.

I long for times
when I felt profoundly
the great loving support
of everyone and everything.

But hear me when I say
that those times I long for
were most often preceded
by some personal tragedy,

followed by a prolonged period
stumbling through darkness.

And those who refuse
to venture into the dark,
will never fully experience
the beautiful and breathtaking
lightness of being.

Other Voices

*I try to see the lightness of life,
and that comes from having a hard time growing up.*
~ Motsi Mabuse

April 12

EXPOSED
A poem for a pandemic.

Into every lifetime
an icy wind will blow

down from the mountaintop,

sweep across the open water,

and leave you standing naked,

so that the birds, bees and trees,

and all nearby will take notice,

as they turn to each other
declaring triumphantly,

We knew it all along!

Just maybe,
this will be enough
for you and me
to finally realize
how fragile we are.

As we dress again,
let us consider each item
we will wear:

Is it necessary?

What does it conceal?

*Has my own nakedness
revealed this world to me anew?*

Other Voices

Illness strikes men when they are exposed to change.
~ Herodotus

April 13

LAST NIGHT
...I slept terribly.

I laid awake for hours
worrying about everything
that will surely happen
but in unexpected ways.

Anxiety is paralyzing.
It shortens my breath,
suffocating my soul.

If I can't breathe
then my soul can't sing
and bring me back
into a peaceful sleep
with timeless hymns
that sweetly remind me
everything is exactly
as it should be.

Other Voices

*A crust eaten in peace
is better than a banquet partaken in anxiety.*
~ Aesop

April 14

APPROACH GOD
...carefully.

The wise know
you'll need just a taste,
and that long before
you open your mouth
God will likely devour you.

The further removed you are
from the day you were born,
the easier it is to forget:

God does not dissolve into you;
instead, you will merge with God.

Like the flame of a candle,
you came here to burn
and offer light to the darkness
before being extinguished
by the breath of the eternal.

Other Voices

There's only one effectively redemptive sacrifice,
the sacrifice of self-will to make room for the knowledge of God.
~ Aldous Huxley

April 15

IT'S SO EASY
...to solve others' problems.

I should know,
I did it all the time.

I mean I provided solutions
others could use or discard.
It was really up to them
to take my good advice.

Fixer, pundit, diagnostician,
these have been my roles for years,
and I was trained into them
by the finest practitioners.

It was an easy life,
though boring and repetitive.
Then came the day I had to resign,
as I was overcome by uncertainty.

You've probably heard:
To solve others' problems,
you have to know them better
than they know themselves,
and be certain this world
is at your control.

Other Voices

*If I knew for a certainty
that a man was coming to my house
with the conscious design of doing me good,
I should run for my life.*
~ Henry David Thoreau

April 16

BELLY FAT
Some may be inevitable.

I want to live inside
the heart of Rumi,
to hear the voice that speaks
only when I am silent.

I want my soul to know
I can feel its subversive hands
steering me in directions
my mind would never go.

I'm ready to lose
that stubborn belly fat,
a symbol of my empty desire
for an easy, unfettered life.

My days are mixed up
in obligation and absurdity.
But at night, just before waking
is when I travel great distances.

I step into an empty boat,
but I am not alone.
I ask, *Who are you?*
Let go of the rudder, they reply.

Other Voices

A fat stomach never breeds fine thoughts.
~ St. Jerome

April 17

YOU WON'T BE PRESIDENT
...and I won't be either.

President is not who we are
and not what we're about.

More importantly,
it's not one of the roles
we're destined to play.

There was a time
teachers told their students,
becoming the president
was the most anyone could
ever hope to achieve.

They told little girls and boys
of all aptitudes and characteristics
they, too, can be president.
But this is simply too limiting,
and shrinks the world of possibilities
just as it begins opening to them.

Maybe you don't agree.
That's fine by me.
But then I'd ask you,
Why aren't you president?

Other Voices

Scrubbing floors and emptying bedpans has as much dignity as the Presidency.
~ RICHARD NIXON

April 18

US
...in love and marriage.

She leaves.
I stay at home.

We'll both travel
great distances in time,
through both work and words,
before coming back together again
to break bread and recount our day.

What is a modern marriage
without traditional roles,
without any children,
without the same old answers
to the same old questions?

As I hear her car pull away,
I pause to say a prayer
and ask for a blessing,
come what may.

Other Voices

*When marrying,
ask yourself this question:*

*Do you believe that you will be able
to converse well with this person
into your old age?*

Everything else in marriage is transitory.
~ FRIEDRICH NIETZSCHE

April 19

HERE AND EVERYWHERE
Let us go there for peace.

One day before
tomorrow.

One day past
yesterday.

There, in-between,
rests today.

Right here is where
I become angry
when you tell me
there is no hot or cold.

I assure you,
I am hot.

*Who is behind this voice
trying to calm me down?*

It seems as though you want
the whole world to remain asleep.

Yes, there may be peace
right here in the present.
But there is also peace
up ahead and far behind,
within the icy outer reaches,
and the fiery furnaces below.

Isn't it the job of prophets
to remind us repeatedly,
peace is everywhere?

Other Voices

*We can never obtain peace in the outer world
until we make peace with ourselves.*
~ Dalai Lama

April 20

AN ARTIST'S PRAYER
...to be filled with abundance.

Please listen to my lament.
See whether these words
may open and bloom,
turning into a beautiful song.

I am tired,
oh so tired,
like a dry river
who's given all his water
to the thirst sea.

The snow will melt
and the rains will return,
but there's little I can do
to hasten them along.

Night after night I pray,
opening my heart to the stars above.
In the wind I feel the hand of God
slowly moving water this way.

Other Voices

*Abundance is a process of letting go;
that which is empty can receive.*
~ Bryant H. McGill

April 21

DARK WAS THE NIGHT
Find within you that light.

Hold still
and you will witness
great beauty everywhere,

all around you,

as it enters your soul,
breath after subconscious
breath.

You will also see
resistance,
heartbreak,
and brokenheartedness,

all of it human,

all of it a valiant effort
to resist wrestling
with our dark angels.

Something in you opens,
then closes upon remembering.

We all shudder
at the ways you have suffered.

Please go to the mat with your demons.

We are praying with you
constantly.

If you die
we will die with you.

Other Voices

*One does not become enlightened
by imagining figures of light,
but by making the darkness conscious.*
 ~ Carl Jung

April 22

THE INFINITUDE
...of love and being...

There's just enough of me
and just enough of you
to go around, even though
we alone are not infinite.

Some days I cannot tell
whether my glass
is truly half-full,
or half-empty.

I wonder:

*Am I pouring my life
into the infinite?*

*Or is the infinite
pouring into me?*

I woke last night
frightened by the dark,
in which the infinite seemed
to be staring right at me.

When I woke again
morning had come,
and the darkness lifted
to reveal my finite world.

Other Voices

*We must learn to reawaken and keep ourselves awake,
not by mechanical aid,
but by an infinite expectation of the dawn.*
  ~ Henry David Thoreau

April 23

THE PATH OF DESCENT
Ten years and counting...

Ten years ago
I made a wise choice,
with my only remaining option
being to turn my will over
to the God of my limited
understanding.

I told myself euphemistically
this would be an inspiring jaunt,
and I smiled brightly as I waited
to be lifted light as a feather,
on a breeze of serenity.

My path began on a Thursday,
at an old limestone church
in a gentrifying neighborhood
of a well-known Texas town.

I parked beneath
a great moon tower,
the arc lights now replaced
by blinding halogens.

Then I entered the church
through an inconspicuous door,
and followed a dark hallway
until I saw a glowing room.

Inside, I found empty chairs
inviting the weary and wary
to begin the long journey
on the path of descent.

Other Voices

I am not alone in my tiredness or sickness or fears,
but at one with millions of others from many centuries,
and it is all part of life.
  ~ Etty Hillesum

April 24

JUBILEE
The year at the end of seven cycles.

*It's time for a Jubilee.
Wouldn't you agree?*

I'll bet it's been
a millennium or longer
since our last one.

Jubilee is a celebration,
a time to let go completely
of all that's holding us back,
while allowing breathing space
in which everyone is set free
to manifest those divine gifts
passionately calling each of us
to become who we're meant to be.

Jubilee reminds us
this world is not rational,
and our enlightenment
must not confine us
within our limited senses,
deep inside an ivy prison
built to enshrine our knowing.

Jubilee is the name
for a universal God who
creates light in the darkness,
strikes a chord in the silence,
wets our lips with wine,
reminds us to forever
dance,
Dance,
DANCE!

Other Voices

I was once like you, 'enlightened', 'rational',
I too scoffed at lovers.
Now I am drunk, crazed thin with misery -
No-one's safe! Watch out!
    ~ RUMI

April 25

LEARNING TO FLY
Coming down is the hardest thing.

Would it be such a shame
if the sober got drunk
and we all did nothing
but lay around for a while?

Turn off your mind.
You don't need it
once you've climbed
the mountain.

But to get back down
you'll need to ask
a child how to fly.

They know how easy
sprouting wings can be.
There's no need to worry
about the size or shape.

They simply watch,
then act like a bird.

Other Voices

*Heaven forbid, everyone might become happy
doing basically nothing
except to lie around and get zonked out on the
wonder of our being.*
~ HAFIZ

April 26

THE VIRUS
...takes on many shapes.

Oran,
Wuhan,
New York
or Dayton...

Did the virus originate
in only one place and time?

The mind says yes,
but the heart knows better.

Plague is an old story,
written into the fossil record,
coded into our DNA,
whispered like a rumor
passed from tree to tree
by the slow breeze
needing to exhale.

A fungus killed the Gros Michel banana.
Dutch elm disease wiped out forests.
And now the Emerald Ash borer
feeds its away across the land.

Covid-19 reminds us
suffering is the pandemic.

Other Voices

...it waits patiently in bedrooms, cellars, trunks, handkerchiefs and old papers, and... perhaps the day will come when, for the instruction or misfortune of mankind, the plague will rouse its rats and send them to die in some well-contented city.
~ Albert Camus

April 27

FEEL THE WEIGHT
It's trying to tell you something.

My soul is heavy.
I know because
I carry him with me
day in and day out.

My heavy soul
enjoys a little levity,
springtime weather,
laughing and playing.

But my heavy soul
is also a remorseless realist,
ever reminding me life is hard
as it steers me toward my pain.

My heavy soul
never tells me to fix,
to try and control,
or to avoid.

Rather he tells me
to witness and show others,
*the cure for the pain
is in the pain.*

Other Voices

*The cure for the pain
is in the pain.*
~ Rumi

April 28

KEEP YOUR PENNIES
...you'll need them for the journey.

Keep your pennies.
Hold on to your thoughts.
Pay attention to your feelings,
and don't barf them everywhere
in your pain, fear and hostility.

I care,
and I believe
we all care
so much
for others,
for the Earth,
for meaning,
for knowing
what it feels like
to be loved
for no damn reason.

Your anxiety is real.
God is anxious too,
and has chosen wisely
to confide in you.

There are places
and there are people
who will listen to you
and know how to live
in the darkness.

Allow them
to accompany you
on your journey
to a greater love.

Other Voices

And what I am beheld again
What is, and no man understands;
And out of darkness came the hands
That reach thro' nature, moulding men.
   ~ Alfred Lord Tennyson

April 29

EMPTINESS
...carves our existence from our love.

Don't waste another day
trying to convince me,
trying to convince yourself,
there is only one right way.

God does not care
how you got there,
only that you go there.

But I'm not suggesting
the end justifies
any means.

Rumi told me
we carve our existence
from our love
for the emptiness.

One day the emptiness
will again appear on the horizon.

This is when
your suffering ends
and your soul
is set free.

Other Voices

Praise to the emptiness that blanks out existence...
Praise to that happening, over and over!
~ RUMI

April 30

SHOULD I BE WORRIED?
Nope. My soul's on duty.

I just woke up
and right away I go
gettin' all worked up,
blockin' the flow of energy,
tryin' to silence the spirit voices
now singing sweetly to me.

They call to my soul,
but I tell them he's not home.

They call again,
and I refuse to answer.

They call again,
so I shoo them away.

How many times
can I refuse these holy spirits
before they quit calling?

Then my soul declares:

*The spirits haven't gone anywhere.
They're right here with me.*

Other Voices

Sometimes I'm more stubborn than I am smart.
~ PAT SUMMIT

MAY

May 1

WE CAN'T GO BACK
...though I'm sure we'll try.

We can't go back.

The illusions we held
in that precious old vase
now shattered on the ground
have scattered everywhere.

There will be blame.
There will be denial.
There will be darkness
and dismissal.

But there will be no way
to put Humpty-Dumpty
back together again.

So long as profit
is the only basis
for life and living,
suffering will reign.

Yet a new day dawns,
filled with possibility
provided we don't retreat
to where this all began.

Ask Elizabeth Taylor.
Ask Richard Burton.
They each married
five or more times.

We can all chase,
but never go back again.

Other Voices

All of our reasoning ends in surrender to feeling.
~ BLAISE PASCAL

May 2

WOULD YOU CHANGE
...if you saw the face of God and love?

You already know
I'm one of the prickly people.
You've heard my confession
and I make no excuses.

But also, like you,
I'm not one of the truly awful,
angry, hostile, vindictive, sad
and deeply wounded people.

I am fortunate.
I've been humbled.
And I am grateful
not to be saddled
with such a weight
as that cruel pain
carried by too many
of our brothers and sisters.

Acceptance,
honesty,
sharing,
confronting,
not resisting,
patiently waiting,
are all powerful tools
of transformation.

Hugs,
inclusion,
forgiveness
and genuine love
also go a long way
in bringing people back
from the depths of trauma.

And still there will always be
a few who must leave this life,
then enter into the next,
before there will be any relief
for themselves and others,
upon whom they inflict
even greater suffering.

The best wisdom I can share
is that which was given to me:

Admit your own suffering.
Confront your own pain.
And don't be any worse
than a little bit prickly.

Other Voices

I imagine one of the reasons people
cling to their hates so stubbornly
is because they sense, once hate is gone,
they will be forced to deal with pain.

~ James Baldwin

May 3

IMPERFECTION
...frames the house of humility.

Wherever did I get
the idea anything is perfect?

Nowhere in my world
am I able to find anything
perfectly round,
perfectly square,
or evenly balanced.

My friend Tom went out
in search of the perfect leaf
but couldn't find one.

Lots of folks seek out
the perfect place to live,
yet never get there.

Even the prefect couple,
in the perfect marriage,
can't always make it last.

Everything surrounding me
is a little bit crooked,
bent, chipped and scratched.

But that aging man
staring back in the mirror
is growing more perfect
in his humble acceptance
of all life's imperfections.

Other Voices

*All imperfection is easier to tolerate
if served up in small doses.*
~ WISŁAWA SZYMBORSKA

BULLSHIT JOBS
...abound.

There's plenty of work,
yet still too few jobs
paying anything more than
the cost of doing them.

Look around.

See all the busy work,
the minimum wage positions,
the service jobs with hard ceilings
and nowhere to go but skid row.

Most blame the workers,
not the economic system
creating these bullshit jobs
that hold so little purpose,
and insufficient remuneration
to support even the individual
doing all the work.

It's truly a disgrace
to our so-called enlightenment;
we cannot see our busy work
is destroying this planet,
while also creating disparities
threatening our very existence.

How have we forgotten
that to be human
is to be of this Earth,
and not simply on it?

Before work
was an empty obligation,
before work defined us,

there was a simpler doing
that could be cruel and mean
and only about survival.

But it led us to this day
when we may now consider
endless new possibilities
for the ways we want
to work and live.

Other Voices

*It's hard to imagine a surer sign that one is dealing
with an irrational economic system
than the fact that the prospect of eliminating drudgery
is considered to be a problem.*
  ~ David Graeber

May 5

MY FAST
...includes a prayer.

I'm getting hungry -
been fasting for three days
with two more to go.

I fast for health reasons,
but am finding there's more to it
as each day goes along.

I've never worried
about my next meal,
yet I worry endlessly
about work and money,
about growing older
and becoming less able
to face the harsh realities
of this mean world.

I also fast to give my body
a break from continuous digestion.

Now as I enter ketosis
I'm starting to notice
a keener sense of smell,
and my heart is saying:

*You can make this fast sacred
by holding it in solidarity
with the poor and the suffering.*

Other Voices

*We observe that in the scriptures,
fasting almost always is linked with prayer.
Without prayer, fasting is not complete fasting;
it's simply going hungry.*
~ JOSEPH B. WIRTHLIN

May 6

ONLY MY SOUL
(THE WAY IS LOVE)
...speaks the mystics' language.

Who speaks to you?

*I mean, who is it
that can cut through the crap
and speak to your soul?*

In the silence
I am mincemeat.

*I declare, Thank God
my soul won't listen to me!*

Like a flower turning toward the sun,
my soul comes to attention
when Rumi speaks.

Please don't repeat my mistake,
thinking that you know
what the mystics are saying.
Only the soul speaks their language.

I told you,
I am only meat.

My journey lengthens
when I am self-centered.

The way is love.

Failing that,
I go with empathy.

Other Voices

The Mystic ascends to the throne in a moment; the ascetic needs a month for one day's journey.
~ RUMI

May 7

WHEN ALL THIS IS OVER
...we really can't go back.

When all this is over,
we can get back to doing
what it was we were doing.

When all this is over,
we can get back to being
who we thought we were.

When all this is over,
we can keep on listening
to the same divisive voices.

When all this is over,
we can try to forget
our love and empathy.

When all this is over,
we can again ignore
death is always nearby.

Or,

when all this is over,
we can sigh a deep breath,
say a prayer for the departed,
and let go of our stubbornness
as we acknowledge our fear
this will never be over.

Other Voices

*God knows when the end of time will come,
not some fanatic...
The world will end someday
but the end of the world and the end of time
are two different things.*
~ DOLLY PARTON

May 8

BELLYACHE
Or is it bellyaching?

Sometimes it takes
a terrible stomach ache
for me to wake up and realize
it doesn't matter very much
if I manage to run errands,
or even get anything done.

At this point of my fast
I was hoping for something else,
maybe a lasting serenity
or some meaningful revelation,
but not with this churning gut.

Sooner or later we all get
a bellyache of our own making.

About all we can do is wait
until the time we may eat again.

Other Voices

*God is day and night,
winter and summer,
war and peace,
surfeit and hunger.*
  ~ Heraclitus

May 9

JOKER
Isn't it beautiful?

>Melissa and I
>watched *Joker* last night.
>
>Afterward,
>my neck and shoulders
>ached with a dark empathy
>for all the Arthur Flecks
>lost in this world.
>
>I know, I know,
>I'm not supposed to feel
>any empathy for a killer,
>even if he is a protagonist
>and suffered profoundly
>when just a child.
>
>It speaks volumes to me
>about our failing hearts,
>that a story so relevant
>to the misery of our time
>must be thinly veiled within
>a blockbuster movie,
>for anyone to even notice
>what the hell is going on.

Other Voices

*Is it just me,
or is it getting crazier out there?*
~ ARTHUR FLECK (JOKER)

May 10

OFF-CENTER
...is where we awaken.

I draw a circle on the ground,
then step inside and wait.

I delay as long as possible
before stumbling out,
unable to hold the center.

I draw a larger circle,
and then another,
before yet another.

I'm forever waking
at the edge of my being
ready to topple over,
under, through, out,
into a larger sphere.

...

My friends,
I offer you what my life
has shown to me:

The center never holds.

It
never
holds.

Other Voices

Nature is an infinite sphere
of which the center is everywhere
and the circumference nowhere.
~ BLAISE PASCAL

May 11

DIVINE RIDDLES
...fill the spaces in-between.

I sit here well-fed,
with no greater purpose
than to become present,
available to send and receive
transmissions of love.

To say I am restless
is like calling the ocean deep
while drifting in a tiny boat
safely on the surface.

Over and over
I ask myself
what to do.

Over and over
the silence urges me
to stay connected.

I never grow tired
of the metaphors and riddles
through which the divine speaks.

Instead,
I grow drunk on them,
wrestle with them,
fall off of them,
sleep and wake up
right next to them,
grow gentle and calm
as I collect them.

Other Voices

*Be silent as a compass, the King
has erased your name from the book of speech.*
~ RUMI

May 12

WHAT ELSE
...have I resisted knowing?

I beg God to please
spare me the details.

I think I've heard everything
and probably know too much
about what doesn't matter.

That damn voice
always telling me I *must*,
does not originate
from the sun or moon,
and is not carried
on the songs of birds
by a strong wind.

A recent rumor
grabbed my attention.
(Silence will always
spill the beans.)

Everyone has a second soul
we gift to our Beloved.

Now here's another thing
I must remember to ask God:

What else have I resisted knowing?

Other Voices

*Fate leads him who follows it,
and drags him who resists.*
~ PLUTARCH

May 13

TO ASH, TO DUST
Is this a dream we're in?

I watch my little dog sleeping
and I wonder achingly,
Why can't he live forever?

I scratch my chin and sigh…

It's easy to see my silly questions
come from an irrational mind
longing for rationality.

The liquids inside of me
are potent and magical.
So how is it we can find
such simple explanations
for what they do?

None of us seems to grasp
the magic contained within
each and every little drop
of a living being.

…

I wrote a poem while asleep.
Most of it went wherever dreams go.

I do remember looking up,
seeing a thousand flickering lights
like sunlight through autumn leaves.

Slowly the lights became glass beads
hanging from a giant chandelier,
and sleeping right beneath
was my little dog.

...

*Allow your dreams to guide you
into the infinite space of forever.*

Other Voices

*The soul, which is spirit, cannot dwell in dust;
it is carried along to dwell in the blood.*
— Augustine of Hippo

May 14

THE MORE I LEARN
...the less I know.

The prophets are gesturing
for me to grab my notebook
and to share with you
what they've just told me.

I started our conversation
by saying to the prophets:

It's getting harder to know
the more I learn.

It's getting more difficult
for me to climb up that ladder
I once believed would deliver
my soul to God.

And as I grow in uncertainty,
I'm curiously more at peace.

Then the prophets said to me:

*Once you know this,
there's nothing else you must do.*

Other Voices

*I took a test in Existentialism.
I left all the answers blank and got 100.*
 ~ Woody Allen

May 15

AS I UNDERSTAND
...*God.*

> I know you
> can see it clearly,
> but I don't want to be
> reminded I am not God.
>
> Sometimes I like to forget
> and go about my day
> as if I had total control,
> always knowing exactly
> just what to do.
>
> I have several ways
> of setting myself straight,
> the most effective of which
> is to recall someone I don't like,
> and then to remember God
> has no problem loving him.

Other Voices

Heaven means to be one with God.
~ CONFUCIUS

May 16

UNTIL NOW
…as is always the case.

Don't look at this day
from the daunting perspective
of what you hope to do.

Go ahead and forget everything
you already struggle to remember.

Deep inside you is someone else
who knows what needs doing
and will warn you if you stray
too far from the course.

In a long and busy life
confusion will always ensue,
as seasons meld and blend
into what must surely seem
like the longest day of your life.

But at the other end
of a lengthy exhale
will be an awakening.

On that new day
you'll reach into your pockets
and find them stuffed full
of invitations to places
you could never imagine,
and would never have gone
until now.

Other Voices

*There is never time in the future
in which we will work out our salvation.
The challenge is in the moment;
the time is always now.*
  ~ JAMES BALDWIN

May 17

MOON HANGING
...behind the art is a wisdom...

A distant poet
sings to the moon
he's placed in one
of a billion night skies.

Until just now I'd forgotten
how many skies there are,
and how many faces glow
upon the moon's surface.

I've been ready
to let others decide
in which night sky
to hang my moon.

I've been ready
to bury my starry soul
beneath the busy work
I thought I must do.

Let's go back to dreaming
about all the celestial bodies
and all those distant skies,
overwhelming the limitations
of what we once thought
it meant to be alive.

Other Voices

*When you feel your lips becoming infinite
and sweet, like the moon in a sky,
when you feel that spaciousness inside,
Shams of Tabriz will be there too.*
    ~ Rumi

May 18

MONEY CONFUSION
No one is immune.

Be aware
and beware
the easy
and not so easy
solutions.

What gets fixed today
falls apart tomorrow.

No one is immune
to those big ideas,
so easy to grasp,
impossible to let go.

Are you crossing your fingers
and suppressing a smile
when you declare,
Not guilty!?

Ours is a world
of trade-offs and causality,
everyone and everything
pushing and pulling
in every direction
simultaneously.

Other Voices

Capitalism has destroyed our belief in any effective power but that of self-interest backed by force.
~ GEORGE BERNARD SHAW

May 19

ZOMBIES
...are life without soul.

Anger and fear
are not the same thing.
Don't confuse the two.

I once thought anger
was the more powerful.
But I was dead wrong.
Fear trumps anger.

Take zombies for example.
Who are the zombies?

Are they only symptoms
of a pandemic virus?

Why are they undead,
so angry and relentless?

Look a bit closer.

Zombies embody the fear
of a world awash in inequality,
where laws and cultural norms
and outright repressive violence
are no longer able to contain
the enemy at the gates.

Pogo once said,
*We have met the enemy
and he is us!*

More specifically,
he is our inability
to confront our fears.

Other Voices

There are things which a man is afraid to tell even to himself, and every decent man has a number of such things stored away in his mind.
  ~ Fyodor Dostoevsky

May 20

HEADLONG
Only fools rush in.

Upon waking today
my soul urged me softly
not to rush headlong into
my usual work and worry,
but rather to take each step
mindfully, allowing this day
to patiently guide me.

My mind protested immediately
with a laundry list of tasks,
and plenty of rational reasons
for me to attack the new day.

But my heart and gut
aren't so easily persuaded,
and firmly refused to listen
to the tyrant in my head.

I waited patiently,
knowing storms do pass,
and a peaceful new day
may emerge in their place.

Other Voices

*I never rush myself.
See, they can't start the game without me.*
~ Satchel Paige

May 21

FIRMLY GROUNDED
...in body and being.

I'm sitting downtown
twenty stories in the air,
so close to the edge,
next to a large window
but with curtain drawn,
in an atrium-style building.

Though I can't see it,
only inches away stands
a two-hundred-foot drop.

So here I am
on a real precipice,
yet completely at ease.

As someone who loves
being grounded on the Earth,
this does make me wonder
about those many times
I've been close to the brink
but had absolutely no clue,
as I sat firmly grounded
in body and being.

Other Voices

*I always liked characters
that were more grounded in reality.*
~ CLINT EASTWOOD

May 22

WE ONLY SEE
...what we're shown.

You and I notice
what we're apt to notice
from our experience,
from our conditioning.

Isn't this too obvious?
Like knowing you're apt to catch
what you set out to hunt,
or will eventually arrive at
the destination toward which
you've always been heading?

I've become attuned
to pain and suffering
because I was offered pain
to acknowledge my suffering.

Believe me when I tell you
pain and suffering are everywhere:

in the men vying for control,
in the women struggling to survive,
in the children screaming for attention,
and in the animals without refuge
as our home is being destroyed.

Yet even amidst
such devastating pain
and overwhelming suffering,
there is abundant evidence
of love and tenderness
still able to sustain life.

Other Voices

We are never so defenseless against suffering as when we love.
~ SIGMUND FREUD

May 23

BEDEVILED
...by my so-called moral life.

I am bedeviled
by the idea of too much,
as others must be
by too little.

I crave balance
between needs and wants,
as I cling to the razor's edge,
so close and always ready
to peel away the flesh veneer
on my so-called moral life.

How can I convince you
of my overwhelming thirst
when you see me drowning
in a sea of human bounty?

I already know -
I have too much.

I already know -
I do too much.

I already know -
I can't live perfectly.

And I already know -
it's okay not to know.

Other Voices

I balanced all, brought all to mind,
The years to come seemed waste of breath,
A waste of breath the years behind
In balance with this life, this death.
  ~ WILLIAM BUTLER YEATS

May 24

ONE LIFE
...but we get to share it.

It takes more than time.

It also takes more than
a supple mind and a satchel
made heavy by life experience.

It takes even more
than your failure to love,
or become something other
than a stoic witness
to birth and death.

It takes a conversion,
a reclamation of the holy,
and wholly innocent, spirit
who bravely accompanied you
on your journey into this world
and now resides at the core
of your human being.

The spirit wants nothing more
than for you to experience God
everywhere and in everything.

You and me
and everyone else
are the simple poets,
singing from the fossil record
this universal truth:

One Life.

Other Voices

*One is still what one is going to cease to be
and already what one is going to become.
One lives one's death,
one dies one's life.*
~ Jean-Paul Sartre

WE'RE ALL IN THIS
...together.

We are
all in this together.

How else could we be?

Haven't you already tried
to step outside and into
something other?

Where did you go?

What did you learn there?

How did it feel?

Did you get lost,
forgetting the way home?

Or have you tried to stay there?

Have you now come back?

Truly?

Is that you I'm seeing –
the same you who left?

Or is it a new you,
made different
by separation,
by solitude,
by humility,
and by the revelation
we're all in this together?

(Are you still hungry?

Are you still homeless?

Are you still having trouble accepting
we're all in this together?)

Other Voices

Two such as you with such a master speed
Cannot be parted nor be swept away
From one another once you are agreed
That life is only life forevermore
Together wing to wing and oar to oar.
    ~ Robert Frost

May 26

THE ETERNAL JOURNEY
...I've always been seeking.

I don't know
if it was always so,
but it seems as though
you and I will only grow
through finding meaning
in our human being.

I was married once
but to no avail.
So I married again
while out on that trail
which leads beyond
all understanding.

Now my day begins,
and will just as soon end,
with that same old prayer
for peace and safekeeping
along this eternal journey
I've always been seeking.

Other Voices

The feeling remains that God is on the journey, too.
   ~ Teresa of Ávila

May 27

POLITICS
...are often best left at home.

Today at the funeral
I left my politics at home.

I can't fool the dead
with my criticism and sermons
about the state of this world.

And I'm sure those grieving
don't need me or anyone else
to analyze or issue judgment
on the life of the deceased.

I just sat in church quietly,
participated in the liturgy,
and paid my last respects
as I listened and laughed
at the funny remembrances
of family members.

That afternoon
upon leaving the cemetery,
I felt a bit lighter,
I felt less alone,
and was really glad
I left my politics at home.

Other Voices

*The largest party in America, by the way,
is neither the Democrats nor the Republicans.
It's the party of non-voters.*
~ Robert Reich

May 28

OUR CELLS
...keep us from growing.

Don't be caught inside
a room with no windows
and no doors through which
you may wander outside.

Once you're trapped
it's so hard to break out.
Most of us soon stop trying,
slowly dying in our cell.

But not you!

You won't be seduced
by simple answers,
or hardened by fear
into a caged beast.

You know love comes
in infinite varieties,
and the way to grow
is out in the open.

Other Voices

*I went down to the prison in Menard,
thinking we were the vanguard,
but down there, I got down on my knees
and listened and learned from the people.*
~ FRED HAMPTON

May 29

TRY NOT TO FORGET
...you always bring yourself along.

Congratulations!

You survived,
made it to this today
relatively intact and hopeful
for a better tomorrow.

You paid a steep price
to unlearn and to unravel
the twine of your existence
into a single golden thread
now connecting your heart
directly with God's.

Who,
seeing you now,
would not agree
you've become
a new man,
a new woman.
a new person,
bowed yet unbroken,
truly beloved?

The time has arrived.
Your bags are packed.
You're now ready to leave
for a new dimension of being.

Other Voices

*Transformation literally means
going beyond your form.*
~ WAYNE DYER

May 30

I HAD TO DIVORCE
...to appreciate marriage.

There came a point
when my education
mattered much less
than my ability to let go
of reason and rationality.

Like the unwinding of a clock,
it took regression and simplicity
to unravel the knots in my head
and restore blood flow to my heart.

I had to release
my drive for perfection
to understand good enough.

I had to realize
even well-meaning people
can inflict unintentional harm.

I had to grow
in order to shrink
to my proper size.

I had to love,
then suffer a great loss,
to make my love stronger.

I had to lose faith
to discover an infinite trust
in a God beyond comprehension.

And I had to die
a thousand times
to truly begin living.

Other Voices

For those who believe in God, most of the big questions are answered. But for those of us who can't readily accept the God formula, the big answers don't remain stone-written. We adjust to new conditions and discoveries. We are pliable. Love need not be a command nor faith a dictum. I am my own god. We are here to unlearn the teachings of the church, state, and our educational system. We are here to drink beer. We are here to kill war. We are here to laugh at the odds and live our lives so well that Death will tremble to take us.
~ CHARLES BUKOWSKI

MY SOUL LIFTS
...when I let go.

The very real strain
of carrying way too much
responsibility for rectifying
the state of the human world
has long burdened my soul
and kept me sober.

Pause to rejoice
if you ever find me
laughing and drinking,
as such silly activities
have always seemed
like mere distractions.

For so long I've despised
and judged even more harshly,
those appearing unable or unwilling
to undertake a bit of introspection
for the benefit of everyone else.

But who am I to decide?

The only way I will lighten up
is by letting go of everything
over which I have no control.

Other Voices

Of all men's miseries the bitterest is this:
to know so much and to have control over nothing.
  ~ HERODOTUS

JUNE

June 1

AROUND THE BEND
...you must go...

Look both ways.

Your life is a road
moving in many directions.

Mother Earth bends,
twists, turns, and wrinkles
the path as you travel.

The wind will blow you
back and forth until
you're completely unsure
which way to go.

But do keep going.

There's something to your life
contained in the movement
and in the unforeseen potential
to collide spectacularly with
the sole purpose of your soul.

Other Voices

*Service to others will help you become deaf to a voice
inside of you that does not believe in happiness...*
 ~ Hafiz

June 2

NEWTON'S CRADLE
For every action, there is...

Why is it
when I push,
you resist,
and when you push,
I resist?

This great energy
embodied in our being
actively imposes itself,
or passively holds the line,
over and over again
trillions of times each day,
all while keeping our world
in a precarious stalemate.

It took only one step
for me to realize,
what I resist persists.

But only after the twelfth step
did I come to realize
that by letting go of my will,
an infinite energy
would flow through me.

Other Voices

*The best criticism of the bad is the practice of the better.
Oppositional energy only creates more of the same.*
  ~ CENTER FOR ACTION AND CONTEMPLATION – CORE PRINCIPLE #3

PREACHER MAN
...all fire and brimstone...

As a young man
I would often play
the part of a preacher,
all fire and brimstone,
and just about as certain
as the day is long.

But I wasn't even remotely aware,
as I stumbled along in darkness,
how near I'd come to the precipice,
nor of all the horrors I'd avoided
by nothing more than dumb luck.

Now initiated,
I can see that any man
not willing to yoke his passion
to a healthy fear of God
is likely to wreak havoc
under the guise of free will.

*(When you see my dad
you might want to thank him
for his time in the seminary.*

*His sojourn in the priesthood
almost certainly spared this world
from me becoming a preacher.)*

Other Voices

*I have so many opinions about everything
it just comes out during my music.
It's a battle for me. I try not to be preachy.
That's a real danger.*
~ Neil Young

June 4

BE RELEASED
...of everything.

I can empathize.
I know the desperate feeling
of being trapped in a moment
with no answers or assurance
of an easy way out.

I could tell you the story
about a crisis at my office
requiring an armed guard
to secure the main entrance.

Or I could speak of divorce,
sitting alone in my apartment
listening to the passing traffic
oblivious to my suffering.

Throughout it all
the Earth kept turning,
each day followed by night,
as these and other crises
would come and go.

. . .

Tell me,
when at a funeral
have you ever dared
to look more closely
at the corpse?

Don't they appear
to be more at peace
than during the struggle
to continue in this life?

I truly believe
it must be this way,
because there is always
and without exception
a much greater peace
in letting go.

Other Voices

*Death is a release from the impressions of the senses,
and from desires that make us their puppets,
and from the vagaries of the mind,
and from the hard service of the flesh.*
   ~ Marcus Aurelius

June 5

A GOOD SIGN
...a man has changed...

I tell you,
it's a good sign
when a man is resigned
and says with a shrug,

*There's nothing else
I must do.*

It's also a good sign
if he's eager to chat,
gives and receives hugs,
speaks when spoken to,
falls silent mid-sentence
and admits he doesn't know.

I'd readily agree
this may seem a bit strange
to those of us grown accustomed
to loud voices and heavy hands.

Still, I assure you
it's a very good sign
when a man stops
whatever he is doing
and asks sincerely,

What is my life about?

Other Voices

*A sudden bold and unexpected question
doth many times surprise a man and lay him open.*
~ Francis Bacon

June 6

REVERENCE FALLS
...like soft rain in the dark...

All the same stories
I've been telling myself
about you,
about those years
now passed behind us
like dust blown down
an empty road –

maybe they aren't all true.

Who will ever know
what happened back there?

Somehow
I became humble
when suddenly faced
by what really matters.

My anger tries to remind me
I never really mattered to you.

Everything we left behind
is still hot to the touch.

Foremost, I remember
our bottomless need.

Other Voices

*When you have really exhausted an experience
you always reverence and love it.*
~ Albert Camus

June 7

HUNTED
We're all prey in a digital world.

My heart is my wilderness,
a natural and evolving place
where rationality is consumed,
the scraps then blown away
by a howling arctic wind
reminding me that peace
will never come easy
in a world designed
to inflame my passions.

When I close my eyes
I can hear my beating heart
advancing on me slowly,
like a relentless army.

From the distance comes
the bay of a hungry wolf.

Startled,
I blink my eyes open
to see him staring right at me.

Other Voices

Men have become the tools of their tools.
~ Henry David Thoreau

June 8

A LONG RELATIONSHIP
…has many secrets to share.

"There were others,
three others to be exact.
But his wife of seventeen years
was the only woman able
to nail him down."

I raise my glass
and salute the happy couple,
but soon begin shaking my head,
recalling those damned promises
presented to me like the gospel
for my own life and marriage.

I seize this opportunity,
presented in a familiar scene,
to reflect on my past relationships,
yet only discover exit strategies
and a much younger man
unable to surrender.

Other Voices

*Like everything which is not
the involuntary result of fleeting emotion
but the creation of time and will,
any marriage, happy or unhappy,
is infinitely more interesting than any romance,
however passionate.*
   ~ W. H. Auden

June 9

SHOW UP
...and be grateful.

Please allow me
a few words of advice
collected from my own
humble experience:

Go
when and where
you're invited.

Then show up
by trying to meet
the expectations
of those present.

Be yourself.

Trust you are welcome
because of the gifts
you alone bring.

There's no need
to shine brighter.

There's no need
to say more.

There's no need
for a good reason.

Just go when called.

And be grateful
for the invitation.

Other Voices

When 'happiness' eludes us - as, eventually, it always will - we have the invitation to examine our programmed responses and to exercise our power to choose again.
   ~ RICHARD ROHR

June 10

WHAT I'D SAY
...to the sixteen-year-old me.

That's easy.
I'd say little or nothing.

Besides,
to my recollection
he doesn't much like
being told what to do,
and could never understand
why all the older men he knows
are grumpy and half-dead.

He'd probably see me
exactly the same way.
And it frightens me
that he might be right.

I'm often irritable,
defeated and bewildered,
unsure what to do next,
if anything at all.

I guess I'd probably try
to show him a smile,
tell him a dirty joke
and remind him failure,
or even walking away,
are possible options,
but love will always be
the only conclusion.

Other Voices

*After adolescence,
if one's life is sufficiently interesting,
the desire to tell oneself stories diminishes.*
~ Gore Vidal

June 11

I NEED YOU
...to need me.

I'm not so sure
that I always say yes,
but I rarely say no
loud enough.

This is how I end up
involved in all sorts of things,
taking on the full charge
and feeling overwhelmed
with responsibility.

Be careful of opportunities
you didn't readily seek out,
with goals and objectives
that come to mean more to you
than the folks who set them.

Ask yourself over and over,
What is mine to do?

Then forgive yourself
if you've done too much.

And for God's sake
stop doing whatever
makes no sense.

Other Voices

I don't want to take too much responsibility, where I'm like, 'Oh, I'm representing Asia.'
~ Lee Chae-rin

June 12

EMPTY CUPBOARDS
I gave everything.

This time around
it took nearly five years
for me to empty my cupboards.
I thought I'd saved plenty,
but now it's all gone.

I suppose it was inevitable
for me to share everything I had.
Besides, I needed to free up space
and make room for some more.

But I did what I so often do
and gave away too much,
without holding any back
for me to rely upon.

So now I'm staring
at my barren shelves,
wondering and amazed
this could happen again,
hoping I won't need
to go the same lengths
to fill them up anew.

Other Voices

When the belly is empty,
the body becomes spirit;
and when it is full,
the spirit becomes body.
~ Saadi Shirazi

June 13

WITH NO WIND
...we must wait.

Hoping for the answer,
Now,
I ask the wind,
When?

But the wind is silent.
Not even a blade of grass
betrays the stillness.

Friends,
now's the time for questions
with no expectation of an answer.

Now's the time to let go
of what's holding on to you.

Now's the time to do
no more than needs doing.

The wind will return soon enough.

Now
is
the
time
to
w-a-i-t.

Other Voices

*We must let go of the life we have planned,
so as to accept the one that is waiting for us.*
~ JOSEPH CAMPBELL

June 14

COMPASSION
...for myself...

Mirror or no mirror,
it's incredibly difficult
to see ourselves clearly.

In a world designed
to reflect and reinforce
who we think we are,
our true self falls
ever further behind
a great façade.

Someone once told me
I'm neither good nor bad,
but rather a complex being
capable of responding
with the best or the worst
of what's within me.

I don't know about you,
but I find it liberating
not to judge myself harshly,
to reclaim my true self
through new opportunities
to deliver the very best
I have to offer.

Other Voices

*Let us fill our hearts with our own compassion -
towards ourselves and towards all living beings.*
~ Thích Nhất Hạnh

June 15

TESTIFY!
I need your witness.

All reason is in revolt!

My soul bribes the bailiff,
who comes to release me.

At my interrogation
I am asked why it is
I demand reason.

Timidly, I respond,

*Is it reasonable
to accept poverty,
to accept torture,
to let people die,
to destroy this planet,
to go on with living
as we've lived for too long?*

Who can argue
with reason?!

Reason grounded in reality
never fails to destabilize us.

Other Voices

*I do not feel obliged to believe that the same God
who has endowed us with sense, reason, and intellect
has intended us to forgo their use.*
~ GALILEO GALILEI

June 16

WRONG OR RIGHT
Which is it?

There's something wrong,
but no one wants to hear this.

There's something wrong,
yet I can't put my finger on it.

There's something wrong,
and I need to look away
to recall what's right.

My life is good.
My work is good.
My health is good.
My marriage is good.

I have a dog.
I have a house.
I have caring friends.
I have a loving family.

So why is it
I feel so uneasy,
as if there's something
seriously wrong?

Could it be because
there's so little I can do
about others' suffering?

Maybe it's because too few
will talk openly and honestly
about what really matters.

Maybe it's because
we're all feeling
afraid and helpless.

Or maybe
it's just because.

Other Voices

*Wrest once the law to your authority.
To do a great right, do a little wrong,
And curb this cruel devil of his will.*
   ~ William Shakespeare

June 17

A LITTLE SUFFERING
...may be necessary.

I'd rather you
keep on struggling,
than me trying to fix
what may not be broken.

There's a kind of awakening
that only comes through toil,
and no one has the right
to deprive you of what may be
a little necessary suffering.

While the struggle never ends,
there will one day come a time
when the crusade against,
and the resolve to fight,
to avoid and to fix,
will cease.

At that hallowed moment,
a strange yet agreeable peace
will settle upon your soul,
quite suddenly you'll see
the sanctity in all other life.

Other Voices

My life is a struggle.
~ VOLTAIRE

June 18

A LOVE LETTER
...to myself...

You're tired,
exhausted,
spent and needing
time away
from everyone,
from everything
now clinging
to your sense
of obligation,
responsibility,
duty and determination
to do the right thing
for love of family,
of community,
of country,
and perhaps secretly,
for the love of power,
prestige and property.

I don't think it's your fault.

What has pushed you
to the precipice of burnout
is the fear of falling behind,
and the obvious wear and tear
of all those precious years
spent racing around foolishly.

But that's no longer possible.

The truth of your life
has caught up to you.

Other Voices

*An idea, to be suggestive,
must come to the individual with the force of revelation.*
 ~ WILLIAM JAMES

June 19

SAVE ME
(Something always does.)

It seems like something
always comes to the rescue.

The second grade saved me
from having to repeat the first.
Songs on the radio saved me
from the darkness of adolescence.
Spring training often saved me
from a seemingly eternal winter.

Even as I grow older,
a savior always comes along,
whether that be new scenery,
marriage, separation, divorce,
loss of all certainty and reason,
or a new love come to reclaim
my wounded soul.

I wonder if towards the end
there will be much left
out there, still able
to save me.

Other Voices

*I know for sure that love saves me
and that it is here to save us all.*
~ MAYA ANGELOU

June 20

DOING LESS
...creates so much more.

What's troubling you?

Me?
I find it awfully strange
the only answer,
to nearly every question,
seems to be more.

The faces I see suggest
we're all wanting a swift end
to this dystopian nightmare,
or are happily living an illusion
and don't ever want to wake.

Brothers and sisters,
I say beware the billionaires
and their legions of admirers.
They call exhaustion progress
and have grown fat and scornful
by adding fuel to the forces
sowing fatigue and discontent.

Become present in your body
by quieting your racing mind
and expanding your heart
with the full range of emotion.

There may yet be a way out,
a way under and over,
or a way through.

It all begins with doing less.

Other Voices

Happiness is not a matter of intensity
but of balance, order, rhythm and harmony.
  ~ THOMAS MERTON

June 21

YOUR ANGER
...needs release.

I am all heart,
the one setting the fire
between your temples,
making you sweat,
making you clench
fist and jaw.

Why do you struggle
to contain me?

You see me in the mirror
and know that I am true,
that I am righteous
and here for good reason.

I might agree with your argument
the head can say it more calmly.

But I must refuse to be
contained here forever
by your empty promises
to finally set me free,
or by you withdrawing
into the silent prison
of an imaginary world.

I need you,
and you need me,
red hot and raging.

I will light the way
through the dark night
to the peaceful resting place
you so deeply desire.

Other Voices

A man who has not passed through the inferno of his passions has never overcome them.
~ Carl Jung

June 22

TEMPTING FATE
...by playing with fire...

    Have you ever pushed,
    poked and prodded
    until you woke a demon
    who burned down your house?

    Like a piano player
    thrashing the keys,
    I search for new chords,
    frustrated yet knowing
    there must be some more
    out there and in here.

    I can't stop
    pushing buttons,
    poking at people,
    prodding the lazy.

    I may be flirting
    with some new demons,
    but I've broken through before,
    and there's something in me
    longing to go back.

Other Voices

...Most dangerous
Is that temptation that doth goad us on
To sin in loving virtue...
    ~ WILLIAM SHAKESPEARE

June 23

NOT VOTING
...also sends a message.

I suppose I'll vote,
but without compelling reasons
I can't seem to muster
a patriotic sense of duty,
obligation or honor.

I'm tired of stories,
imagined and embellished,
cynically goading me toward
sympathy and nostalgia,
anger and animosity.

Sadly, these days
voting is much more about
money and manipulation
than a sense of duty
or public service.

Am I angry?!
Aren't you?!

I'm not saying
don't vote.

I'm not saying
it doesn't matter.

I'm not saying
the struggle for voting rights
should be forgotten.

I'm just saying
it's a valid third option
not to vote.

Other Voices

*If you think you can slander
a woman into loving you,
or a man into voting for you,
try it till you are satisfied.*
    ~ Abraham Lincoln

June 24

I KEEP ON WRITING
...in league with my soul.

I cautiously read back
the words written for you,
afraid of what I might find
hidden in the phrasing.

Everything I write
starts innocently enough,
with only the best intentions.

Yet sooner or later,
I discover a man speaking
with a foot firmly in his mouth.

Still I keep on writing,
to remind myself it's okay.

I keep on writing,
to remind myself I'm alive.

Then I keep on writing
to remind myself this endeavor
is forever a work in progress,
and that even the Gospels
struggle under scrutiny
to satisfy the fickle mind.

Other Voices

*In the realm of ideas everything depends on enthusiasm...
in the real world all rests on perseverance.*
~ Johann Wolfgang von Goethe

June 25

THE SPECIALIST
...learns through repetition.

My prayer today
is that I've learned most,
if not all, of the very real
and very sober lessons
I needed to learn.

But I don't doubt
there's much more
I'll need to know
before I go.

My list is long
of repeated mistakes,
and is well-documented
by family and friends,
by all the scars I wear,
and even a court decree.

Time is always too short
to go on lamenting the past.
So I'm trying to live for today
as I remember to keep asking,
Have I done this before?

Other Voices

*Specialists are people
who always repeat the same mistakes.*
~ WALTER GROPIUS

June 26

MY LIFE STORY
For whom is it written?

Who's the story teller
telling me my story?

The last time I checked
it was me writing that book,
busily scribbling the finale
to my triumphant mythology.

But that was years ago.
I've since burned those pages
and started taking dictation
each and every morning
from my shrewd soul
and the panoply of spirits
with whom I sit in council.

I'm no longer certain,
as I live more fully my true life,
that it reads like a story.
It might make better sense
sung by a forgetful romantic
as an old folk song.

Other Voices

When you come across a storyteller
Know a house is being destroyed.
   ~ Rumi

June 27

THE PERFECT SPACE
...exists alongside our imperfection.

Why does it surprise you
to learn you're not perfect?

If you'd give it some thought
you'll see perfection is subjective,
and that the unattainable ideal,
perhaps instilled by mom or dad
or by the world in which you live,
is akin to fashioning wings
so you can fly like a bird.

Let those wrinkles around your eyes
become the cracks in your certainty.

Stand up straight.
Relax your brow and your fist.
You'll need to draw a deep breath
after receiving this gut blow.

Maybe today you can begin
living within your imperfection,
and thus tomorrow life and love
may flow freely through you.

Other Voices

You will never be happy if you continue to search for what happiness consists of. You will never live if you are looking for the meaning of life.
~ Albert Camus

June 28

CHANGE OF HEART
It just takes a beat.

There comes a point
in every child's development
when he begins to recognize
his being is also physical,
and she can repeatedly
impact her environment
in all sorts of fun ways.

It starts innocently,
perhaps with throwing a ball
over and over again.

Slowly, this realization
becomes fixed in the psyche,
as the child grows larger
by pushing further out
and into the world.

This outward push continues,
perchance until a brush with death
or some other awakening comes,
when the forgotten child realizes
her true impact on the world
can be magnified and multiplied
by redirecting that outward push inward
toward a change of heart.

Other Voices

In the divine milieu,
all the elements of the universe touch each other
by that which is most inward and ultimate in them.
There they concentrate, little by little,
all that is purest and most attractive in them without loss
and without danger of subsequent corruption.
   ~ Pierre Teilhard de Chardin

June 29

MORNING BELL
...release me.

The new day always comes
too often and too early.

In the distance
just before daylight,
I can hear a bell tolling,
as if slowly saying,
more, more, more.

More seems like the truth,
but I know it's really a lie
I've only been repeating
and wanting to believe.

Each night I drift off
to God knows where,
but just before waking
I realize I'm in my attic
filled with so much junk
I don't need anymore.

In the moment I don't know
what to do with all the crap
I've saved and accumulated,
but as I look into the boxes
everything just goes away.

When I got up this morning,
I discovered a truth hidden
in one of those boxes I had stored:

*The purpose of my life is
to hold and lessen all the suffering,
beginning with my own.*

Other Voices

*I continue to be drawn to clarity and simplicity.
'Less is more' remains my mantra.*
~ Stéphane Rolland

June 30

STOLEN VOICE
...an ode to silence...

I inhale slowly,
then push the air upward,
over my vocal cords.

But all that comes out
are some pops and squeaks,
like an old and favorite song,
familiar in tempo and tenor
yet missing the expected notes.

Who or what stole my voice?
I honestly don't know.

If it's an infection,
it lacks a fever and congestion.

If it's acid reflux,
I'm not experiencing heartburn.

If it's the climate,
I can't remember better weather.

What could it be?
Stress? Strain? A virus?

I never fully understood
the power of a voice
until I lost mine.

Other Voices

*Silence is as deep as eternity,
speech as shallow as time.*
~ Thomas Carlyle

JULY

July 1

WEARY CONFESSION
...from a little traveler...

I like to think
little frightens me.

By now I do know my death
may happen very suddenly
and I'll have no time for fear.

Or it may unfold more slowly,
at which time I may struggle
to remain present.

Either way, my life has been
a series of sober discoveries,
a long, winding journey through
the narrow twists and turns
of celebration and tragedy.

But I must confess,
what frightens me most
is the evident accumulation
on my body of wear and tear,
which, with each passing year,
is unable to endure the same
stress and physical beating
I once thought it could,
and no longer wishes
to go to battle in vain.

Other Voices

*People do not seem to realize
that their opinion of the world
is also a confession of character.*
~ Ralph Waldo Emerson

July 2

HESITATING BEAUTY
I saw my heart break in two.

*What have you learned
that keeps you alive?*

Let's get out of the way,
the clichés and easy answers,
like your love for family,
doing some good for others,
and especially that ardent desire
to make the world a better place.

Authenticity requires honesty,
the kind that rips through flesh
like the blade of a serrated knife
and exposes the unconscious.

Go outdoors at night.
Sit in a room full of strangers.
Visit the grave where you buried
those memories and experiences,
or even that nameless person
too painful to carry with you.

So here's my answer:

I must remind myself often,
it's okay to be broken.

My scars are the currency
I use to negotiate my way
with all sorts of beings,
along the silk road of life.

More than anything
I wanted to win.

But more importantly,
I hesitated to lose.

I can be serious,
and I can be tender.
I can be funny,
and I can be loving.

At last, I can also be alive
without holding on to shame,
and without turning my life
into some kind of game.

Other Voices

If you gain, you gain all.
If you lose, you lose nothing.
Wager then, without hesitation,
that He exists.
   ~ Blaise Pascal

July 3

LITTLE BITTY ME
...struggling toward self-awareness...

Discovering who we are
and what we're here to do
is the spiritual project
of our lifetime.

By this point I know
I'm a little bit nomadic,
a little bit stubborn,
a little more creative
as I struggle to have fun.

I am a little bit tired,
having spent so much time
trying to be heroic.

But I'm also a little bit wiser
for all the roles I've tried on.

I'm a little bit afraid,
and even more courageous.

I worry a little,
but prefer to search
for those bits of cheer
dropped by other people.

I'm a little bit sad
this will all come to an end.

Yet I'm also a bit curious
about what's out there,
waiting for little bitty me.

Other Voices

Self-awareness is value-free. It isn't scary.
It doesn't imply that you will subject yourself to needless pain.
　~ Deepak Chopra

July 4

SOCIALISM
...is in our DNA.

    Sound the alarms!
    Socialism is coming.

    But wait,
    isn't it already here?!

    Medicare,
    Public Drinking Water,
    Public Firefighters,
    Public Airwaves,
    Public Lands,
    Public Museums,
    Public Roads,
    Public Utilities,
    Public Schools,
    Public Zoos,
    Social Security,
    Social Services,
    and let's not forget
    the Veterans Administration.

    Go ahead and scream it.
    Get it out of your system.

    There's no such thing as a free lunch!

    But of course this isn't true.

    You forget that first free lunch,
    enjoyed at your mother's breast,
    and the countless others since.

Other Voices

The New Deal is plainly an attempt to achieve a working socialism and avert a social collapse in America; it is extraordinarily parallel to the successive 'policies' and 'Plans' of the Russian experiment. Americans shirk the word 'socialism', but what else can one call it?
— H. G. Wells

July 5

PANDEMIC
...from pan "all" + dēmos "people"...

A pandemic is
a pointed reminder
there's little time
for us to be bitter
and stew in our anger;
righteous or indignant,
it does not matter.

A pandemic is
not the best time
for despair and dread,
but rather for acceptance.

It's a chance to see life
from a new perspective,
and then to move forward
through cooperative efforts.

A pandemic puts
the brakes on the pushing
toward a punishing probability,
and swiftly changes the narrative
to that of peaceful possibility.

Other Voices

*All things are subject to interpretation
whichever interpretation prevails at a given time
is a function of power and not truth.*
~ FRIEDRICH NIETZSCHE

July 6

THE GEARS
...have stopped grinding.

The world outside
is strangely silent.

There's no whooshing traffic,
and I don't hear the creaking
of school buses braking
at every other driveway.

This must be what
this world sounded like
in preindustrial times.

Each day started
a little more slowly,
a little more quietly,
a little more peacefully.

I didn't know.
We didn't know.

Yet few among us
are likely not enjoying
this rare opportunity
to catch our breath.

In times of real crisis
ideology matters so little.

How will the tycoons
bring their world
back up to speed,
now that we all know
it can be slowed down?

Other Voices

Wisely and slow.
They stumble that run fast.
~ WILLIAM SHAKESPEARE

July 7

FALLING SLOWLY
...into that deep mystery.

>Every little ache and pain
>is trying to tell you something.
>
>But you won't listen to them
>until you've been tripped,
>and while in midair falling,
>are confronted by no ground.
>
>From that point on
>I'm not sure what happens.
>But falling slowly for a bit
>may be a good start.

Other Voices

*In such a porcelain life,
one likes to be sure that all is well
lest one stumble upon one's hopes
in a pile of broken crockery.*
~ EMILY DICKINSON

July 8

DNR (DO NOT RESUSCITATE)
...the old order.

*Doesn't it seem silly
to be talking about money?*

*Zero percent interest rates,
bailouts and quantitative easing,
do almost nothing to address
the real issues we are facing.*

*Most people don't know
how they're going to survive
without income or healthcare,
with children to feed and clothe,
and to care for all day long
because there is no school.*

*The old order is creaking
and leaking fossil fuels.
There's blood on our hands
and bodies in the streets.
Already large parts of it
aren't working at all.*

It's time for something new!

*Aren't you fearful our good faith
will be wasted on a last ditch effort
to resuscitate the old order?*

Other Voices
I was broken beyond repair.
~ Elizabeth Smart

July 9

34
...seemed like a turning point.

Last night I dreamt
I was thirty-four again.
It really wasn't so long ago,
a pleasant age to be.

I had just enough life experience,
which would soon lend itself nicely
to uncovering the wisdom I'd need
for the remainder of my life.

Also when I was thirty-four,
the tide had already begun to turn
on our Twentieth Century illusions
and was headed back out to sea.

I think I knew by thirty-four,
and maybe even earlier
at the tender age of thirty-two,
my radical but ordinary odyssey
was only just beginning.

Other Voices

*We don't receive wisdom;
we must discover it for ourselves after a journey
that no one can take for us or spare us.*
  ~ Marcel Proust

July 10

SHOCK DOCTRINE
Let's make lots of money.

The *Shock Doctrine* says
that no tragedy or catastrophe,
whether natural or otherwise,
ought to be wasted.

Rather, each is an opportunity
to be exploited for dramatic
economic and social change.

Think flood and famine,
hurricane and earthquake,
wars and pandemics,
and the easiest to exploit:
economic collapse.

What will happen
in the days, weeks, months
following a great disaster
all depends on who sees it
as a disguised opportunity,
and what they hope to achieve.

Other Voices

I always tried to turn every disaster into an opportunity.
— John D. Rockefeller

July 11

YOU DON'T NOTICE
...what your soul sees clearly.

Oh, this world!

Even when I focus my attention
I often fail to see what's near to me.

Somehow the awesome beauty
of the blue sky on a summer day
will elude my wandering eyes.

And I may not even notice
the pain and suffering of others
hiding in plain sight.

It seems I only call to awareness
what I want my eyes to see
or my ears to hear.

But bless my soul;
he's a tireless instigator,
randomly knocking on doors,
then wheeling and dealing
with all sorts of shady spirits.

Before too long,
I find myself digging out
from all the wonderful mischief
my soul has invited.

Other Voices

*We do not need more intellectual power,
we need more spiritual power.
We do not need more of the things that are seen,
we need more of the things that are unseen.*
~ CALVIN COOLIDGE

July 12

INSIDE THE LINES
...is where we play it safe.

I'm not sure what to write
because I'm not sure what to do.

This is an unusual feeling.
I readily admit to always holding
some degree of uncertainty,
but it has rarely influenced
how I go about living my life
as I keep to my daily routine.

I suppose I ought to become
better acquainted with this feeling,
especially in a world convulsing
amidst pandemic and transformation.

Both my heart and gut
are reliable and true as ever,
but my mind is wavering
as it tries to keep me
inside the lines.

Other Voices

Cowardice asks the question, is it safe?
Expediency asks the question, is it politic?
Vanity asks the question, is it popular?
But conscience asks the question, is it right?
And there comes a time when one must take
a position that is neither safe, nor politic, nor popular,
but one must take it because it is right.
   ~ Martin Luther King, Jr.

July 13

SACRED SEEDS
…bear a fruit called serenity.

It took a few years before
I could find and cultivate them.

The seeds were patiently waiting
in my heartbreak and sadness.
They germinated in darkness
and began to flourish in solitude.

My questioning and negativity
seemed to be a kind of fertilizer.
Or maybe it was my skepticism,
and all the years of unwept tears
that watered them from within.

I don't know what exactly,
but something made serenity grow
in the barren and empty landscapes
of hopelessness and isolation.

When I returned home
I brought serenity with me.

Amidst a normal life
serenity seems a bit ordinary,
like a common house plant
or lamp in the spare bedroom.

But out of doors,
in our wild animal existence,
serenity flourishes and sustains,
whether it waxes or wanes.

Other Voices

*Your heart is full of fertile seeds,
waiting to sprout.*
~ Morihei Ueshiba

July 14

TINKERER
...sounds so much better than fixer.

Taking things apart is just something I do.
I started with my toys and other gizmos,
then moved on to more abstract things
like culture and the human psyche.

I deconstruct
in order to figure out
just how something works
and hopefully understand it,
with a sincere hope to fix,
or maybe make it run
a little bit better.

But by my age
I ought to have learned
it's rarely a good idea
to analyze other people,
venturing into headspaces
where I know I don't belong.

Other Voices

My wife tells me,
"Terry, tell me what you like about it,
before you tell me what you don't."
     ~ Terry Symens-Bucher

July 15

CASSANDRA COMPLEX
...seeing things others may not wish to...

I heard a wise man,
a well-regarded teacher
and spiritual leader,
confess he can often see
the problem in something
without even trying.

My heart skipped
and I lost my breath
upon hearing these words.

Me too, I thought.
That's exactly how I feel:
Like the priestess Cassandra,
who was cursed by an angry Apollo
for thwarting his sexual advances,
with having the power of prophesy,
and yet no one would believe her.

And perhaps this teacher
would also warn me
that seeing the problem
is really more of a curse,
if first I don't concede
there's truth and beauty
in almost everything.

Other Voices

*Prophesy is a good line of business,
but it is full of risks.*
~ Mark Twain

July 16

WANTING TO ESCAPE
...but with nowhere to go.

My left ear keeps popping,
so I tear a piece of cotton
and put it deep inside.

Immediately my world goes
from stereo to mono
and I feel a little distanced
from all of my senses.

It's allergy season,
but not one like any other.
This is the year of Covid-19,
when any cough or congestion
is confronted with caution
and a raised eyebrow.

I want to get away,
to be far from all of this,
to find a place without allergens,
removed from the restless anxiety
of people sheltering in place.

Other Voices

*What some call health,
if purchased by perpetual anxiety about diet,
isn't much better than tedious disease.*
   ~ ALEXANDER POPE

July 17

THE PANIC ENDS
...when you go into the silence.

I was alone at home
during my first panic attack.
Instinctively, I took my pulse,
placing two fingers on my neck
so I could feel my heart racing.

For the next two years
I would check my pulse often,
desperately needing to confirm
my heartbeat had slowed.

During this period of my life
I kept quiet vigil with the darkness,
and would gladly listen to anyone
who might lovingly assure me
everything that had happened
was relevant to my life.

When I finally saw
a light break on the horizon,
my heart returned to a steady beat.
And somehow I knew to keep still,
letting go of what I thought
remained to be done.

Other Voices

Quietness is the surest sign that you've died.
~ Rumi

ENJOY THE SILENCE
...for the greater good it brings.

I hope you can hear
the humility in my words.

I've often confused action
with doing something;
moments when the greater force
would've been my stillness.

If I can offer some advice
to myself and anyone listening,
it would be:

There are times
to do absolutely nothing
until the act of doing merges
with the reason for your being.
Then you know profoundly
what must be done.

Other Voices

*The near stillness recalls what is forgotten,
extinct angels.*
~ Georg Trakl

July 19

A POINT OF VIEW
Everyone has one.

My dog knows things
I will never know.

He smells things
I didn't know held a scent.

He sees this world
from only twelve inches
above the ground.

When he hears something
deep within the silence,
I watch him tilt his head
to listen more closely.

You and I are human,
but we too absorb this world
from various perspectives.

We frequently notice
what the other does not,
and react to worldly stimuli
with distinct sensitivities.

It's a wonder
we agree on so much!

Aren't you amazed
we made it this far together,
living in a subjective world
with all of our relationships
mediated by the senses?

Other Voices

Our subjectivity is so completely our own.
~ Spike Jonze

July 20

LOVE CHANGES
...everything.

My time is better spent
walking and relating,
cooking and caring,
humming and sitting,
than in worrying too much
about the fate of this world.

My spiritual rehabilitation
exposed my buried soul,
which then leapt from the depths
and angrily slapped me silly.

My soul demands:

Who are you?
Where are you going?
What are you doing?

You never slow down
and listen to me or to God.

Your superego is just another voice
echoing inside of your head.

Don't remain angry
because you fooled yourself
and can now see others
doing the same thing.

Unleash your madness!

What you don't know
and are afraid to find out
is how love changes you,
and in so doing, changes
how you see this world.

Other Voices

*That is the real spiritual awakening,
when something emerges from within you
that is deeper than who you thought you were.
So, the person is still there, but one could almost say
that something more powerful shines through the person.*
 ~ Eckhart Tolle

LIKE A ROCK
...but not quite so firm...

I'm beginning to wonder
whether I've become a stone.

I often fear the world
right outside of these walls
where I live and work.

And there are many days
when I'd rather be indoors,
though I can never resist
my fearless little dog
urging me to venture out.

Still I feel heavy,
and like a great rock,
resistant to being moved
by all the commotion
surrounding me.

I now hear chants coming
from distant monasteries
and the swirling wind whistling
through empty hermitages...

Aren't you also witnessing
the great forces now gathering
to move the unmovable?

Other Voices

You are always a student, never a master.
You have to keep moving forward.
 ~ Conrad Hall

July 22

UNITIVE LOVE
...the real, real thing.

Love without cause
is the real thing.
It is more eternal
than any rock
you can build upon.

The stuff you must earn
is not true love.
So don't try peddling it
to God or to anyone else
who knows the real thing.

It almost seems silly
for me to mention
something this central
to the creation of our Universe,
but for the fact that as humans,
we must devote our lives
to the task of rediscovering
the inherent and unitive love
which connects us to everything.

Other Voices

*One of the main tasks of theology
is to find words that do not divide but unite,
that do not create conflict but unity,
that do not hurt but heal.*
     ~ Henri Nouwen

July 23

GRACE
...is felt in timeless gratitude.

A morning prayer
for Grace -
that conscious letting go
into the weightless feeling
of being lovingly held,
which seems to arrive so easily
in those vast spaces
glimpsed from mountain tops
and along the ocean shore.

Grace requires stillness,
deep and easy breathing.

Grace fills the emptiness,
satisfying my needing.

Grace is the forgiveness
I struggle to offer.

Grace is knowing
all is as it should be.

Grace is accepting
a beginning without end.

Let us come to Grace
by way of quiet invitation
into an open mind
and a surrendered heart.

Other Voices

*Grace is everywhere as an active orientation
of all created reality toward God.*
~ KARL RAHNER

July 24

MY GRIEF
...suppressed will suffocate me.

Why is it so difficult
for a man to name
what he is feeling?

He must learn
everything is not anger,
frustration, rage,
or jealousy.

Right now
I'm feeling sad,
grieving really.
But it took me a while
to figure this out.

Others,
nameless people in photos,
men and women sharing
their own stories of grief,
helped me to feel my own.

So now I weep
way down in the deep
for the way things are,
for the inexplicable losses
I can't possibly define,
and for my own complicity,
albeit somewhat innocent,
in my own grief.

Most of all
I grieve my impotence
to do anything about my grief,
except to grieve.

Just as there's no way
for me to exit this life,
except through the body
in which I came into it,
there's nothing beyond my grief
unless I go through it.

Other Voices

*Grief can be the garden of compassion.
If you keep your heart open through everything,
your pain can become your greatest ally
in your life's search for love and wisdom.*
    ~ Rumi

July 25

SOBRIETY
...may surprise you.

Who but the unfortunate
grow up stone cold sober,
and therefore only anxious,
about the brutal,
yet also beautiful miracle
it is to be alive?

The fortunate man or woman
drinks for good reasons,
though eventually learns
continuous drinking
only keeps them drunk.

The cure for drunkenness
is not simply to recognize
everyone is drinking.
Rather, sobriety begins
when a third eye opens
and beholds the infinite
within this strange reality,
as well as the hopeless futility
of trying to escape.

Other Voices

*Years ago I used to commiserate
with all people who suffered.
Now I commiserate only with those
who suffer in ignorance,
who do not understand the purpose
and ultimate utility of pain.*
 ~ BILL W.

A TOOTHACHE
...is but a dentist's unwritten poem.

    Lying in the chair
    listening to my dentist,
    I begin to doubt
    his love for poetry.

    And yet he's in possession
    of sufficient heart and mind
    to sing and dance,
    to drill and fill,
    and to do whatever
    his patients need done.

    For me, a toothache
    is a long pause
    between lovely verses.

    For him, a toothache
    is a blank page,
    and his drill full of ink.

Other Voices

*There are men so philosophical
that they can see humor in their own toothaches.
But there has never lived a man so philosophical
that he could see the toothache in his own humor.*
    ~ H. L. Mencken

July 27

SINUSITIS
...ya know it if you've had it.

Half of me is inflamed
while the other half is wondering
what the hell's the matter.

I thought fire burned evenly,
but it's become obvious enough
this crazy world is filled
with unevenly charred matchsticks
and half-baked human beings.

Like a pair of glasses missing a lens
I'm having trouble finding my focus
or even knowing what to look upon.

And just as fog spills
haphazardly into a valley,
so too does the cement
hardening in my head.

Other Voices

*Life is better when your sinuses are clean,
when your arteries are clean,
and when your digestive tract is clean.*
~ JAMES ALTUCHER

CRAWLY THINGS
At last I can see and hear those spirits

I should have trusted all along!
I just killed an ant
right beside my chair.
But don't worry,
there are many more.
All around us live
some unseen millions
of tiny crawly things.

Wise voices assure me
these ants and spiders
now wrinkling my brow
and giving me the shivers
may be something more
than they appear to be.

I suppose nothing crawling
could ever fear the soil.
And as I've learned to live with fire
by being gentle with fire,
I may learn to love this Earth
by accepting everything
which comes from Earth.

Other Voices

Love makes your soul crawl out from its hiding place.
   ~ Zora Neale Hurston

July 29

WHAT FEEDS ME
Is it sediment or sentiment?

Far from perfect, unless
perfection is really its opposite,
I've become a membrane
allowing the rich sediment of life
to pass right through me
while absorbing what feeds me.

Other Voices

*Skin is not only an envelope protecting the inner body,
or a membrane that allows exchange
between exterior and interior of the body.
It also serves as a mingling point
between the outer world and inner self,
and between body and soul.*
   ~ Miru Kim

GOOD FORTUNE
...is being here, now.

If you see me,
would you remind me
of my good fortune
at being born here and now,
in this time and place
and not some other?

And please help me
to appreciate my experiences,
as well as all those things
unique within my manifestation
of human being.

It's so easy
for me to drift away
into the hollow longing
for another time and place.
But the real gift within my soul
is the presence to be here now.

Other Voices

*It is we that are blind,
not fortune.*
    ~ THOMAS BROWNE

July 31

WHAT BECKONS
...is calling you forth.

This morning I sit
in my tiny log cabin
somewhere next to I-70
in Southern Illinois.

I can hear the trucks
barreling down the wet asphalt,
already late to St. Louis.

I also hear birds in their nests
chirping breakfast orders
to other birds flitting about.

Outside it's drizzling,
cool but not cold.
Inside I make tea
to warm and to wake.

I think I'll sit and wait
for the hour to call me forth,
as I count all the spiders
and begin to plan my day.

Other Voices

When love beckons to you, follow him,
Though his ways are hard and steep.
And when his wings enfold you yield to him,
Though the sword hidden among his pinions may wound you.
  ~ Khalil Gibran

AUGUST

August 1

MY LAUNDRY LIST
It's always longer than I thought.

Today I'm feeling needy,
but my real desire is to feel good
so I can be at my best.

And I'd like some courage too,
to do what I've committed to do
while being present throughout.

Some extra energy might also be nice,
because I'm really counting on
my mind and body to last this day.

So here's my laundry list, God.
It's full of prayers and wishes,
along with my sincere promise
to show up no matter what.

Other Voices

Give me a laundry list and I'll set it to music.
~ Gioachino Rossini

August 2

OVER AND AGAIN
...a bit of wisdom from Sunnen Lake.

Wet,
a little bit cold
and a lot tired,
but already
a better man than
when I arrived.

I told myself,
before telling my wife,
I'd come home renewed
and reinvigorated
once I collected
my true self.

Then I often find
I don't have to go so far
away from my home
to gather all the pieces
of my being.

Yet for some reason,
I must make this journey
over and over again.

Other Voices

*Life is a journey that must be traveled
no matter how bad the roads and accommodations.*
~ Oliver Goldsmith

August 3

THE SOUND OF SILENCE
...is filled with soulful voices.

The poetess Meisaan tells me,
God does not close doors to opportunities,
but rather closes them to our excuses.(1)

Then Laozi warns me
not to pick up and wield a weapon,
that in violence every victory is a funeral.(2)

Next Henri laments the world at large,
poised on the brink of nuclear holocaust,
yet finds optimism in so many hope-filled hearts.(3)

I think Hafiz may be right,
we are at a very low tide,
but the water will come back.(4)

While Aquinas is quick to remind me,
we are all madly in love
with the same God.(5)

And from Rumi comes my soul's voice:
When union happens, my speech goes inward,
towards Shams...
When school and mosque and minaret
get torn down, the dervishes
can begin their community.(6)

(1) Meisaan Chan - *Curving Toward the Center* - July 17
(2) Laozi - *Tao: 31st Verse*
(3) Henri Nouwen, *You Are The Beloved*, July 23
(4) Hafiz, *Why All This Talk?*, trans. Daniel Ladinsky
(5) Thomas Aquinas - Attributed Poetry
(6) Rumi, A Year With Rumi, trans. Coleman Barks

Other Voices

Only when you drink from the river of silence
shall you indeed sing.
~ KHALIL GIBRAN

August 4

AT THE CREEK BOTTOM
...I find my soggy soul.

The breeze off the lake
begins to chill my already
rain dampened mood.

But a walk in the woods
is all it takes to rediscover
that missing part of me,
submerged yet still alive
at the creek bottom.

So I fish out my soul,
and in so doing awaken
something deep within,
a little bit frustrated,
and maybe a whole lot angry
about forgetting my belonging
to this natural world.

Now I'm feeling annoyed
and even more uncertain,
as I ponder what to do
with my awakened soul.

*Could this be the Great Spirit
urging me to breathe new life
into all the sleeping souls
I encounter on my journey?*

Other Voices

*Poetry is thoughts that breathe,
and words that burn.*
~ Thomas Gray

August 5

SING
...for the love you bring.

That which has been given
and allows the birds to sing,
now demands for me to sing.
But first I must let go of
silencing my timid voice.

Before I knew I could sing,
even before I knew I must sing,
I realized my life would eventually
be determined by my letting go.
Release after unfathomable release
of all those many songs
I am both aware and unaware
I cling to desperately.

Now I frequently try to sing,
and I'm sure others have heard me
thinking, he's still got much to let go.
But I hope they can also hear
my quivering voice gaining strength
the more I am able to release.

And as I sing this song
I realize I must be careful
and not let go too quickly,
slipping into that dimension
the birds always trill about.

Other Voices

*What was said to the rose that made it open
was said to me here in my chest.*
    ~ RUMI

August 6

SALTWATER
...a frightening cure.

Tears launch me into
that ocean called feeling,
my emotions like waves
threatening to subsume me
in their salty waters.

No sooner am I castaway,
adrift in my tears
and fearful of everything
swimming down below,
than I begin to look for dry land
rising out of the depths.

Like the fisherman of yore
I set out on a turbulent sea,
then reel myself back in before
I become too heavy and sink
in a saltwater grave.

Other Voices

I suppose I've always done my share of crying, especially when there's no other way to contain my feelings. I know that men ain't supposed to cry, but I think that's wrong. Crying's always been a way for me to get things out which are buried deep, deep down. When I sing, I often cry. Crying is feeling, and feeling is being human. Oh yes, I cry.
~ Ray Charles

August 7

HEALING MODALITIES
...are like strings on a guitar.

There are so many
healing modalities
with deep, deep roots
in human experience,
and, I would suggest, also
in the understanding
of human pain.

Some modalities may work
much better than others,
but the ones which heal us
as we stumble along
the pathway called life
will become our favorites,
and also the high notes
in the evangelical songs
we sing to the world.

Other Voices

Healing yourself is connected with healing others.
~ Yoko Ono

August 8

THE NOTES
...sometimes summon the words.

This morning I feel as though
I haven't anything profound to say,
and nothing much to share
beyond my frustrated confession.

I've emptied my pockets,
shaken out my shoes,
and checked under the bed.
But there's nothing to report
beyond the expected dust,
a pebble and a lost M&M.

Yet something assures me
it's okay to be adrift
and also a bit anxious,
or whatever this feeling is.

It's like an unfinished song
waiting for words to be added.
Once I've got the notes,
the lyrics soon come.

Other Voices

*I find lyrics can come at any time during the day,
as can music.*
   ~ Hozier

August 9

COMMUNITY
...is the manifestation of true connection.

On the darkest night
I saw a flash of light
as my soul awakened
to birth the poet within.

I dreamt a waking dream
of death and destruction,
then fell fast asleep,
allowing that darkness
to show me the light.

Letting go is not easy.
It requires much more
than a stiff drink,
a shock of gray hair,
or the harsh slap
of bitter reality.

I only began to fall
when I actually fell.
So now when I tell you
I can no longer shoulder
the weight of responsibility
for everything and everyone,
you will know that by stumbling,
I discovered a sincere humility
and a deep desire for community.

Other Voices

The need for connection and community is primal, as fundamental as the need for air, water, and food.
~ DEAN ORNISH

August 10

RELEASING
What it means to die before you die.

Some say it's easy to let go
when the end is near.
I don't know for certain,
but some kind of ending
is fast approaching.

My new beginning
is pointing like an arrow,
urging me into consultation
with my living elders -
into the darkness
and out through light.

Men and women
show me their scars,
and though I cannot see
my own battle wounds,
I must trust I am healing.

I now tell others about
my aching shoulders,
how I can no longer carry
the weight and responsibility
I once gladly accepted.

They laugh and nod,
pour me a drink,
then urge me to rest
while I sit back and enjoy
the relief in letting go.

Other Voices

*Death is a release from the impressions of the senses,
and from desires that make us their puppets,
and from the vagaries of the mind,
and from the hard service of the flesh.*
~ MARCUS AURELIUS

August 11

TELL ME
In Spanish I'd say, "¡Digame!"

Don't bother me with the news.
It doesn't much matter
who said what,
the deal that was struck,
or even the seven-day forecast.

I want to go to that place
where the slow repetition of life
offers me a glimpse of eternity
without the illusion of permanency.

So tell me about your vacation,
how you noticed the tides
and can now recognize rain clouds
amassing on the horizon.

Tell me about waking up
to the chirp of a single cricket,
and how falling asleep felt
no different than being awake.

Tell me that peace is contagious
and beauty is everywhere.
Maybe you can point out other things
I'd also want to see and hear.

Other Voices

Slow down and think about the lessons of the elders.
~ Maya Soetoro-Ng

August 12

TAKE THAT LEAP
Bonzai!

Do you look before you leap?
Or like my Yorkie, Simon,
do you leap and hope for the best?

Whenever and wherever you leap,
I wish you a safe landing.
But don't forget the most important part:
taking that leap.

Other Voices

*All growth is a leap in the dark,
a spontaneous unpremeditated act
without benefit of experience.*
~ Henry Miller

August 13

JOY OF BEING
May you never forget it.

When I was a child,
I remember adults
taking great pleasure
in giving me opportunities
to play and to create
without any set goals, except,
perhaps that I might discover
the inherent joy of being
they once knew intimately,
and never want to forget.

Other Voices

*Memory and poetry go together, absolutely.
It is a matter of preserving and of remembering things.*
~ Lisel Mueller

August 14

BITE YOUR TONGUE
...unless you have something nice to say.

There is no burning desire
guiding my pen this morning.
Maybe it's because the air in here
is too stuffy and would improve
if only I'd open a window.

Ah, now that's better.
Here comes a cool breeze
to remind me of what my dad
would tell his bickering children:
*If you've got nothing nice to say,
say nothing at all.*

And so I gently guide my mind
away from those harsh words
always on the tip of my tongue
and toward a softer language.

I now realize time is too valuable
and life much too precious, to cling
tightly to one or two emotions.
I try to expand my heart
through the effort of falling in love
with this strange and confusing world.

Other Voices

Saying nothing... sometimes says the most.
~ Emily Dickinson

August 15

A BEGINNING'S END
...is just another new beginning.

I don't know where to begin.
I'm no longer even certain
there is a beginning.
Something happened
(*as it always does*),
and now I can see
the beginning of one thing
at the end of another.

I do hope you, too,
can find your way back,
as often as is possible,
to a child-like understanding
that the world is as it is.
You need do nothing
other than be yourself,
in order for love to be manifest
in your precious, tiny life.

Other Voices

*Every new beginning comes
from some other beginning's end.*
~ SENECA

August 16

THE SILVER LINING
...is our capacity to connect and care.

There was a mass shooting
in my city last Saturday night.

Upon learning this news
I became completely numb,
unable to appreciate
the flood of concerned messages
from family and friends.

Because shootings happen,
everywhere and frequently,
to think about this tragedy
made me sigh in resignation,
so certain those dark forces
that foment these massacres
would work diligently to thwart
any collective response.

Yet after a long day
in which I began to feel
the deep pain and sadness
intertwined with the slaughter,
I started to notice and appreciate
the inherent desire deep within
to connect and to ensure
the well-being of everyone.

Other Voices
I came to the plain fields of Ohio with pictures painted by Hollywood movies and the works of Tennessee Williams and Arthur Miller. None of them had much to say, if at all, about Dayton, Ohio.
    ~ Chitra Banerjee Divakaruni

August 17

BEYOND COST
...and any other economic terms.

Because of behavioral sciences
we know it can be costly to change
our habitual ways of thinking.

The cost comes
from the energy and time
it takes us to make that change.
And of course time is money,
the cruelest arbiter of all things.

But who are we
if not change agents,
paying for our tiny lives
with blood, sweat, and tears,
and whatever imagination
we can avoid suppressing?

Cost is an economic term.
When we close our eyes
for the very last time,
what we've paid for our life
will be more than enough
to purchase a first class ticket
into the universe of sublime love.

Other Voices

Both economics and politics are false sciences.
~ Leon Russell

August 18

THE MANUALS
Toss 'em in the recycling bin.

Somewhere,
maybe in a tall glass building,
but certainly in front of a glowing screen,
there's a technical writer preparing
a manual I'll stubbornly refuse to read.

A good manual takes time
and great skill to prepare.
The more complex the machine,
the heavier the manual necessary
to keep things running smoothly.

No offense,
but I don't want to read 'em.
I don't particularly trust anything
too complicated not to be obvious.

In my experience,
the very best manuals contain
simple pictures and drawings,
and never make assembling something
seem too difficult.

Other Voices

Language ought to be the joint creation of poets and manual workers.
~ GEORGE ORWELL

August 19

NOTHING BEYOND LIVING
This is the task at hand.

A voice inside commands:
just sit down and do it.
So I summon the discipline
to sit down and start doing.
Countless others also heed
this same merciless voice,
as all of us seem to be busy
doing a little something.

It starts early in the day
when alarms are triggered.
Next, the water pressure falls
at the nearby pumping station
and the breeze begins to swell
with the faint smell of coffee.
Soon roads will be congested
with the cars of sleepy travelers,
all heeding that stern urging:
it must be done.

Meanwhile, a child watches
as squirrels chase each other
round and round a tree trunk.
Her school bus approaches
but she hears no voice.
She hasn't yet forgotten
only her life is inevitable,
and she's nothing to do today
beyond living.

Other Voices

*My appointed work is to awaken
the divine nature that is within.*
— PEACE PILGRIM

August 20

COME INTO THE LIGHT
...and show us your soul.

I see men and women
wandering a barren landscape,
searching desperately for a flower,
a blade of grass, water, anything
to let them know they are alive.

Why do they shrug
and give up their searching?
Is it because they can find
no way onto their knees?

Grab a shovel and get to work.
Let's uncover a way into
the darkness we've been avoiding.
Let's dig our own graves
and lie down in them,
allowing the damp earth
to show us who we really are.
Let us look up at the sky,
as we accept the invitation
to be born yet again.

Now rise!
Tell us the stories
told to you by the darkness.
Come into the light
and show us your soul.

Other Voices

*In my next incarnation,
I want to be a writer.*
~ FIDEL CASTRO

August 21

TRUTH AND THE SOUL
...are everywhere you look.

Truth is unmistakable.
You will know it,
by the weight
it places upon your chest,
intensifying each breath,
or by the way it strips you
naked of your defenses
with nowhere left to hide.

Truth may be offered
by a friend or foe,
yet always carries
a burdensome load.

You may live in a house
but you must tear it down
to see the sun and the moon,
to feel the wind and the rain,
to understand the truth
of who you really are,
and, by the grace of knowing,
become who you are meant to be.

Other Voices

The truth is incontrovertible.
Malice may attack it,
ignorance may deride it,
but in the end,
there it is.
  ~ Winston Churchill

August 22

FIGURING IT ALL OUT
It must add up to something.

To me, everything
once seemed so innocent,
from a drive along the river
to Grandma's sweet tea.

But as I grew older
life began to feel like a struggle
for which there are no answers,
not even a guaranteed reward.

Then somebody told me
that life's super easy,
so long as you don't try
to figure it all out.

Other Voices

*The first step in solving a problem
is to recognize that it doesn't exist.*
— Anonymous

August 23

CHURCHED
Allow it and it will happen.

I've never had
a church experience
in church.
And I daresay
few have.

Church always finds us
where we need to be found.

Church found me
in countless small rooms
attached to chapels
of all denominations,
where I'd sit in small groups
right beside the Holy Spirit,
which filled all the spaces
between folding chairs.

And I've been churched
in nature's cathedral,
rendered speechless
by the awe of witnessing
my presence and belonging
to the awesomeness
of creation.

And I've been churched
while alone in the dark,
longing for something
to happen.

Other Voices

I believe that God knows what each of us wants and needs. It's not necessary for us to make it to church on Sunday to reach Him. You can find Him anyplace. And if that sounds heretical, my source is pretty good: Matthew, Five to Seven, The Sermon on the Mount.
~ Frank Sinatra

August 24

SHE
An ode to the feminine and beyond...

She is surrounded by fluidity.
Some might mistake it for naivete,
but I say it is an easy acceptance,
a willingness to live with uncertainty.

I, on the other hand, hold suspect
anyone who does not prefer
a certain flavor of ice cream
or a particular Christmas song.

She somehow manages to live
in those nebulous spaces between
the stone columns on the courthouse
and the bodies on a crowded dance floor.

Just getting to know Her
has shifted the center of my being
to where I can no longer focus
my believing on a single truth.

Other Voices

I spent a lot of years trying to outrun or outsmart vulnerability by making things certain and definite, black and white, good and bad. My inability to lean into the discomfort of vulnerability limited the fullness of those important experiences that are wrought with uncertainty: Love, belonging, trust, joy, and creativity to name a few.
~ BRENÉ BROWN

August 25

PRESBYOPIA
With age comes perspective...

Can someone tell me,
does midlife feel
like a fraying at the edges,
a blurring of the near?

At the Iowa State Fair
a reporter asks Joe Biden,
"How many genders are there?"
"At least three," Joe replies.

Once there were two
and now there is no gender.
Or maybe it is three,
a trinity, like Joe says.

Something in me finds hope
in this strange revelation.
Could it be we are becoming
comfortable with ambiguity?

Other Voices

Religious belief has made me comfortable with ambiguity.
~ Richard Rohr

August 26

THOSE WHO SURVIVE
...must be able to adapt.

Those who survive
will be strong and resilient,
uniquely able to tolerate
a harsh and inhospitable climate.
Their DNA will resist
the degenerative effects
of all the synthetic chemicals
spilled upon this planet.
And they will be mentally tough
as they toil for existence
while struggling to heal the scars
from a devastating machine
fueled by our fear and greed.

I want these people to know
we have glimpsed their future,
and there are those among us
much softer and willing to suffer
the great pains of change
with the hope life may continue
for all plants and animals.

We know from experience
there is and will be no utopia,
except for that space within
where we cultivate acceptance
through peace and love.

Other Voices

*I was taught that the human brain
was the crowning glory of evolution so far,
but I think it's a very poor scheme for survival.*
~ Kurt Vonnegut

August 27

WITNESS ME BARGAINING
...with [insert noun here].

Whenever I close my eyes
I become a meditating monk,
tranquil in my heavy robes even though
something is gnawing at my toe.

Am I okay?
I must ask this question
countless times each day,
and more often than not
must accept a dubious reply.
Maybe it's always fear,
which first visits the mind.

Now that I can see,
what is it I'm seeing?
Witness me bargaining
with my human suffering,
wanting to know absolutely
before slowly coming to peace
with [insert noun here].

Other Voices

*There is no witness so terrible
and no accuser so powerful
as conscience which dwells within us.*
~ Sophocles

August 28

WHAT'S THE RIGHT AMOUNT?
Trust your instincts.

What's the right amount
to say and do,
to read and write,
to work and play,
to eat and drink,
to love, love, love
and then let go?

When I wanted to talk,
no one asked me to speak.
Now that I've something to say
I'm reluctant to disturb the peace.

The East calls silence a virtue,
while the West says actions
speak louder than words.
So I've learned to take
the narrow path in-between.
I hold my breath when necessary
and speak when I'm invited.

Other Voices

He that would live in peace and at ease
must not speak all he knows or all he sees.
~ Benjamin Franklin

August 29

A PRAYER FOR EVERYONE
...we among them.

Many among us hold
a thinly veiled ambition
to become better persons
than those we know
or can point to on a screen.
The bar seems always
set beyond our tiny reach,
just outside of what prayer
and faith can attain.

So let's not make
a list of the innocents.
Soon enough the dead,
and even the unborn,
will also run afoul
of our harsh judgment.
Instead, let's say a prayer
for all of the victims,
we among them,
and for all the victimizers,
we among them.

Other Voices

*Through our own recovered innocence
we discern the innocence of our neighbors.*
~ HENRY DAVID THOREAU

August 30

TWICE
...a double lifetime.

I twice read
a book of poetry
because my mind
wouldn't let it all in
the first time.

And if I could live
this crazy life twice,
I'd be grateful to try
and allow more love
to pass through me.

Other Voices

You cannot step into the same river twice.
   ~ Heraclitus

August 31

CHEERS TO THE MISFITS!
...and to the not-so-crazy ones.

I toast everyone
who doesn't quite fit
into the forms we are given,
whether that be a body,
or a job and family,
or a country and culture,
or anything else that won't fit,
like a hand-me-down jacket
or a rented prom outfit.

Don't we all do our best?

First we celebrate change
with games and cakes and parties.
Later we suppress change
with drugs and money and laws.

Those who are enemies of change
create monuments to their resistance,
while everyone else grows slowly
in ever-widening circles of acceptance
until there is no soul left outside
the divine circumference of the universe.

Other Voices

*When you're just like everybody else,
you've nothing to offer other than your conformity.*
~ Wayne Dyer

SEPTEMBER

September 1

SET YOURSELF FREE
...you'll never regret it.

You can light a fuse by listening,
burn down a house
by changing your mind.
You might even save a planet
by letting go of your ideas
and allowing your soul
to speak its truth.

Just because you have money,
a few words, maybe some scars,
and the right kind of anything,
this gives you no special status
in the one true universe.

You know the bargain.
It keeps you awake at night,
setting your mind ablaze
when you brush up against
the pointless confinements
within our meritocracy.

So set yourself free
by doing nothing but
allowing the grace
of your liberated soul
to occupy that space
you're forever trying
to conquer and defend.

Other Voices

*I wish that every human life
might be pure transparent freedom.*
~ SIMONE DE BEAUVOIR

September 2

ROCK
...molten and moving.

What I've found
too difficult to master
is the adamant refusal to change
devised and demanded
by a fundamentalist mindset.

The common thinking holds,
at the heart of all being
is a block of solid granite,
fixed and resolute,
like the will of God.

But the God we meet
in the streets and alleyways
of our embodied lives
hides around corners carrying
all sorts of intriguing gifts.

No one who's lived life
through the portals at their senses
knows rock as anything other
than the tumbling evidence
of our steady yielding
to change.

Other Voices

*I think it's inevitable to evolve
if we allow ourselves.*
~ Alyssa Edwards

September 3, 3019

LOVE
...everywhere and growing.

Some say it in song,
others say it in dance.
Many repeat it in church,
while others whisper it in school.
I like to write it down,
hoping you like to read it.
I know a few who photograph it,
and maybe one or two who paint it.
Almost everyone talks about it,
but no one would describe it the same.
Some might point at the moon,
whereas others feel it in their veins.
You might encounter it in the forest,
or in the excitement of your devoted dog.
Everyone has once glimpsed it
or suffered its gnawing absence.
But it's never gone too far,
only that we stray from the source.
Of course you know what I'm talking about,
you've been wearing it all day long.

Other Voices

*Love is a fruit in season at all times,
and within reach of every hand.*
~ MOTHER TERESA

September 4

HARMONY
...precedes all creation.

I'm calling off the search.
My personal trips to odd ends
of our amazing planet
yield little beyond my humble awe
for the sheer size and beauty
of the fierce and gentle landscapes
continuing to change and evolve
as they slowly give birth
to ever newer forms of life.

Now comes the time for me
to simply be and to discover
my own deeper belonging
in a community called life.
Here competition fades,
taking with it the struggle
to live forever singularly,
thus allowing the possibility
of an eternal life beyond
the grasp of my individuality.

Other Voices

*People crave comfort,
people crave connection,
people crave community.*
~ Marianne Williamson

September 5

THE WINDS
...with all their flapping wisdom.

The song of the south wind
sounds like the voice of a devilish child
taunting me to come out and play.

Yet I only allow myself to heed
the call of the steady north winds
pushing me hard and to the east.

Now I've taken down my sails;
I much prefer to stay put,
out of all the jostling currents.

Still, at night I feel the west wind
creeping through an open window
to remind me who I really am
and what is mine to do.

Other Voices
Who am I to blow against the wind?
   ~ Paul Simon

September 6

NOSTALGIA
...isn't for me.

I've no need for nostalgia.
I see how it whitewashes the past
and creates resentment,
tightening the screws in my jaw
and contorting my fingers into fists.

Not that I don't have fond memories,
wonderful moments I still recall
through the softening filters
and ink-faded colors of time,
which also remove troublesome details
while leaving only positive feelings.

So what are these memories
I'm trying to unearth and preserve
as I dig into the catacombs of my life?

Time is a rock tumbler
and our blood the abrasive,
polishing all of our memories
into the smooth agates
we keep in our pockets
and save for a rainy day.

Other Voices

*Nostalgia is a powerful feeling;
it can drown out anything.*
~ Terrence Malick

September 7

LUCKY
...without rhyme or reason.

>Sometimes you get lucky,
>or maybe even really lucky,
>when a tornado passes by
>right over your neighborhood
>before demolishing the next.
>
>So today I am grateful
>and also a little perplexed.
>Rhyme and reason works well
>in both songs and poems,
>yet manifests a bit differently
>in the world at large.

Other Voices

Luck is believing you're lucky.
~ Tennessee Williams

September 8

DECAY
...just one part of the life cycle.

There comes a time
when a tree can no longer
stand tall as a tree
and falls to the ground.

Likewise a rock
will one day split open
and give itself to the wind,
one grain of sand at a time.

I, too, am being simplified,
broken down at the spiritual
as well as the molecular levels
into my constituent pieces,
each of them a part of the whole.

Other Voices

The fertility cycle is a cycle entirely of living creatures passing again and again through birth, growth, maturity, death, and decay.
~ WENDELL BERRY

September 9

SOUL FOOD
Where do you go to be fed?

I must remember
not to ask so many questions.
The questions and answers
both mean very little
until a man or woman
can no longer remember
all of their yesterdays,
and thus can let go
their absolute certainties
about tomorrow.

Like flags I've seen
flapping in the desert,
our answers are threadbare
until, with nowhere left to climb,
we fall back to our ground.

I like when a weary traveler
seeks me out to ask,
Where do you go to be fed?

Other Voices

*If you can't feed a hundred people,
then feed just one.*
  ~ MOTHER TERESA

September 10

AWAKENED
I hope you weren't sleeping too soundly.

The awakened
make terrible house guests.

They ask for little,
but their very being
demands from you
the kind of attentiveness
which makes it difficult
to sleepwalk through your day.

Imagine the Buddha
sitting at your kitchen table
and silently sipping tea.
His reverence to your hospitality
overwhelms you with gratitude
for the generosity of life.

And maybe Mary Magdalene
confides to your listening
the story of a young man who
seduced her with his passionate heart,
yet needed her feminine touch
to remind him of his humanity.

What then?
Might there be a moment
when the fog of everyday living
lifts to reveal the possibility
you might answer "yes"
to that nagging invitation?
Then you stay awake and begin living
your soul purpose for being.

Other Voices

To be awake is to be alive.
— Henry David Thoreau

September 11

THE POETRY OF FIERCE LANDSCAPES
It's all mirrors.

The poetry of fierce landscapes
lives and breathes a warrior life
in damp overgrown jungles
reverberating with the sounds
of buzzing insects and falling water.

It lives in the high deserts
where stone after goddamn stone
soaks up the heat of the sun
baking out all of the softness,
turning even a gentle heart
into dust on the wind.

It lives in crowded cities,
malignant neighborhoods collapsing,
unable to sustain the weight
of such concentrated need.

The poetry of fierce landscapes
wraps the human heart in vines
and slowly silences beating drums
until the whole world becomes
still, like a panoramic painting
seen from outer space.

Other Voices

*There's a fierce practicality and empiricism
which the whole imaginative,
lyrical aspect of poetry comes from.*
~ DAVID WHYTE

September 12

IF EVER...
Do you realize?

Do the dead smile
when they notice
how much you love
simply being alive?

Is something inside you
deeply rooted and still vibrating
with those kinetic energies
creating this world?

Was there ever a time
you thought you were alone,
but then felt God nudging you
toward an experiential knowing
of your profound belonging?

Other Voices

Color is the keyboard,
the eyes are the harmonies,
the soul is the piano with many strings.
The artist is the hand that plays,
touching one key or another,
to cause vibrations in the soul.
  ~ WASSILY KANDINSKY

September 13

THE CRESCENDO
...that great run of notes.

I've seen a piano with toes
carved on giant claw-like feet,
standing ready and waiting
for that great run of notes
which will loosen its varnish skin,
allowing it to leap from the stage,
and like the specter of a jaguar
paralyze onlookers in their seats.

The gifted virtuoso must then
struggle and fight the beast,
coaxing him back on stage
by soothing the hardwood body,
and gently tapping the ivory keys
so as not to awaken the elephant
in search of his tusks.

Other Voices

Each song is a small universe to me. Each song has a story of its own. Each has a full life to express in order to be complete, so it often happens that the building to a big crescendo feels right in the recording or writing process.
  ~ DAMIEN RICE

September 14

ALL THOSE PLACES
...once thought of as somewhere.

This will be a silly poem.
But sometimes all you need
is just a few simple words,
not too self-conscious,
and not at all concerned
about who won't like them.

So here it goes,
this is my ode
to Wheeling, West Virginia,
to Ashland, Kentucky,
to Portsmouth, Ohio,
to Gary, Indiana,
and to all of those places
once thought of as somewhere,
but that are now an afterthought
except to those souls who
frequent the old McDonald's,
getting to know the characters
from the local cast of life,
lending an ear listening
to the sad soliloquies
of the forgotten.

Other Voices

Somewhere,
something incredible is waiting to be known.
  ~ SHARON BEGLEY

September 15

I USED TO KNOW
I did.

I used to know.
I used to know exactly
what's next,
who to call,
how to get there,
and when to arrive.

All you had to do
was ask me
or tag along.
I'd willingly share
my certainty.

I used to know
because others knew
and told me
what I should know,
what I ought to expect.

Now I admit to you,
I've learned a few things
about knowing and
about not knowing.

You can still count on me
to arrive on time,
but don't be surprised
when I tell you
I don't know.

Other Voices

God is best known in not knowing him.
~ Augustine of Hippo

September 16

A SOFTENING
Let it, and it can happen.

My heart, steadily hardened
through years of resentment,
maybe for some good reasons,
is slowly beginning to soften.

Several days ago,
I attended a funeral
held in an old cathedral,
where I began to notice
the beautiful stained glass,
the vaulted roof timbers
and ornately painted ceiling,
along with all the embellishments
calling me toward a place
of alluring tranquility.

Spending time in nature
accords me similar feelings,
but being in that basilica
gave me pause to think
of my relatives and ancestors
who spent their lives in church,
perhaps one of the few places
in which it was possible for them
to transcend their difficult lives
and go on living each day.

This church or their churches
may not hold the absolute truth,
but at times it probably offers
a glimpse of the same mystery
that leads me to the equanimity
where I can write this poem today.

Other Voices
The end of confession is to tell the truth to and for oneself.
~ J. M. Coetzee

September 17

GRANDFATHER
An obvious source of insight.

It's happening more frequently now.
I'm thinking of my grandparents,
wondering what they were doing
and what they thought about
in their middle years.

In 1953 one of my grandfathers
died in a horrific farm accident.
In 1958 the other grandfather
was my same age now.

It's hard for me to imagine
either grandfather held doubt
about the world he knew,
or was ever uncertain
about his place within it.

Both likely came to understand,
as I'm just beginning to learn,
how unwilling most of us are
to embrace life's ambiguity,
allowing change to overtake us.

The grandfather I knew
lived for forty more years,
long enough for me to witness
the interior distances he traveled
to become an enduring source
of love and generativity.

Other Voices
*You have to do your own growing
no matter how tall your grandfather was.*
~ ABRAHAM LINCOLN

September 18

AMAZING GRACE
How sweet the sound!

Scotland the Brave softens my heart
as does *The Star Spangled Banner*.
Yet neither can summon my tears
like *Amazing Grace* on the bagpipes.

Today there is no flag,
save the white flag of surrender,
which means more to me
than that amazing grace
which saved a wretch like me.

Other Voices

He who learns must suffer.
And even in our sleep
pain that cannot forget falls
drop by drop upon the heart,
and in our own despair,
against our will,
comes wisdom to us
by the awful grace of God.
  ~ AESCHYLUS

September 19

THINGS I DON'T REMEMBER
How the hell did I get here?

This morning
my mind wanders
down corridors,
through catacombs,
unable to find
a quiet resting place.

I'm struggling to recall
the words I've just read.
Only the phrase,
we are all house-sitting,
lingers in my head.

Even though I know
my life is brief,
I counsel myself
to be patient,
especially on days
when I'm lost
and distracted.

Other Voices

Our heart glows,
and secret unrest gnaws
at the root of our being.
Dealing with the unconscious
has become a question of life for us.
　~ CARL JUNG

September 20

SURPRISING
...how the heart changes.

If you live long enough,
again you will be surprised.
I repeat, again and again,
just like way back when
you were a child.

After all these years,
it won't be the thing itself
that elicits your smile
or a tiny eruption of laughter,
but rather your reaction
to the surprise itself.

First comes the time
we expect the unexpected.
Then comes the time
we accept the unexpected,
as our heads and hearts
no longer fear surprise
or need to understand it.

Other Voices

Laughter can bring a new perspective.
~ Christopher Durang

September 21

SILENCIO
It's music for the soul.

Now that I'm listening,
now that I'm paying attention,
the silence speaks to me
like an eighty-piece orchestra.

Sometimes it's like Mozart,
bright and uplifting,
perfect for a sunny day.

At others it's dark and heavy,
like Wagner's swirling Valkyries
on a dark, wintry night.

And then there are moments
when the silence is pure genius,
like the lustful and divine light
pouring from a wounded Beethoven.

I see why some
might avoid the silence.
It's like taking a drink
from a fire hose.

Still the silence feeds my soul,
speaking from deep within
and in-between all the chaos
- a symphony calling me to sanity.

Other Voices

*True silence is the rest of the mind,
and is to the spirit what sleep is to the body,
nourishment and refreshment.*
~ WILLIAM PENN

September 22

TO BE AN X
What's in a generation?

Everyone enters this world
in a generation of one
or of one hundred million.

My generation is called X.
We're like the card burned
before dealing a hand
of Texas Hold 'em.

To be an X means
being squeezed between
two much larger generations:
the Boomers and the Millennials.

To be an X means
arriving at the beginning
of a crumbling world order,
still fully invested in it.

To be an X means
owning a healthy skepticism,
yet unable to avoid feeling
depressed and hopeless.

To be an X means realizing
we're gonna be all right,
even though we must let go
of our youthful expectations.

Other Voices

*Each generation imagines itself
to be more intelligent than
the one that went before it,
and wiser than
the one that comes after it.*
~ GEORGE ORWELL

September 23

MY SOUL IS SERENE
Praise God!

My notebook becomes sacred
the moment I begin
filling up its pages
with mystical words
emanating from my soul.

I hear the word *two*,
then I write the word *lovers*.
Next, I hear the word *death*
and I write the word *doorway*.

My soul comes out of the dark
and into focus as a tree,
as a babbling brook,
but also as a spider,
to keep me a bit uneasy.

My soul is exactly
who I really am.
So my soul is serene,
ever reminding me
everything is precisely
as it should be.

Other Voices

God grant me the serenity
to accept the things I cannot change,
the courage to change the things I can,
and the wisdom to know the difference.
    ~ Reinhold Niebuhr

September 24

INSTRUMENT OF LOVE
...is what you are.

    I want to write
    with a leaping lyricalness,
    an always fresh perspective,
    without anything being pinched
    or the flow held back
    by too much elastic.

    I hear songs
    being sung everywhere,
    at all times
    and in impossible voices
    I could never -
    ever have imagined hearing,
    even if, like the mountains,
    I had a million years
    to sit and wait.

    The notes are in the particulars:
    the who, what, where, when,
    and especially the why.

    The heart says,
    Why do I make music?
    And the soul spirit says,
    Because you are
    an instrument of love.

Other Voices

I regard myself as a beautiful musical instrument, and my role is to contribute that instrument to scripts worthy of it.
~ ED ASNER

September 25

MY FIRST POEM
...is called "Gothic Love."

I often forget
my poetry is me,
naked on this page
- the blood, guts, bones,
and whatever else
my soul reveals to me
when I stop worrying
how I look in the mirror.

I no longer recognize
the vulnerability that I felt
when I shared my first poem.
Yet I remember the place,
a coffee shop in Sacramento.

It took a while for me to summon
the courage necessary to speak.
Afterward, the rush of emotion
compelled me to flee the scene.

Other Voices

*No one can possibly know what is about to happen:
it is happening, each time, for the first time,
for the only time.*
    ~ JAMES BALDWIN

September 26

BEYOND LOVE STORIES
Don't bother holding your breath.

When I am in love
I am teetering on the edge
of something unspeakable,
something unknowable,
something uncontrollable,
something so desirable.

We all speak of falling in love.
I speak to you of love's madness,
of being obliterated by love,
covered by the inky substance of love,
lost in the labyrinth of love,
standing at the rocky precipice
where I still know who I am,
and that great leap of abandon
into the wonderfully infinite
God.

Other Voices

*There are love stories,
and there is obliteration into love.*
~ RUMI

September 27

BREATH
Easy come, so hard to let go.

If you've ever had
your breath knocked out,
you remember the silence
of being in that vacuum
between exhale and inhale,
feeling a great terror
breath might never return.

When breath finally did return,
relief came in huge gulps of air
and a flash flood of emotion,
from the salty tears of relief
to a painful new understanding:
passage between dimensions
may be quite difficult.

Other Voices

A human being is only breath and shadow.
  ~ Sophocles

September 28

MANHOOD
...a journey of descent.

I'm a man
and therefore pretty good
at avoiding and at stoicism,
at keeping a stiff upper lip
while biting my lower one.

I'm willing to say goodbye,
swallow my emotions,
choke back tears,
and take one for the team.

But as I grow older
I have no illusions
about glorious violence.
I don't feel romantic
about days gone by,
or forget all the suffering
caused when men lose touch
with the sacred feminine.

Sometimes I blush
to admit my tenderness,
not wanting to come out
from behind the fallen rocks
along the shores of manhood.

Other Voices

*You seek the heights of manhood
when you seek the depths of God.*
~ Edwin Louis Cole

September 29

POUR
...yourself out.

Fluid,
flexible,
formless,
free and full
of love and ease,
following open paths
through all landscapes,
along life's mysterious edges
where the confluence
becomes ocean,
then jungle,
then desert,
then city,
then a silent starfield
in the darkness of space,
until a shooting star
returns you to Earth,
and to the even flow
of your being.

Other Voices

*Rocks and waters, etc.,
are words of God, and so are men.
We all flow from one fountain Soul.
All are expressions of one Love.*
  ~ JOHN MUIR

September 30

THE REAL THING
...is embodied experience.

There are many things
which can only be known
through experience.

Explanations and metaphors
eventually are exposed
as the threadbare best
anyone can possibly offer
in place of the real thing.

Sunrise in the mountains,
freedom on the open road,
resisting a swift current,
standing before an audience,
the death of a loved one,
your first, very first kiss –

all mean so much more
to the embodied soul
than they ever could
to even the most earnest
of intent listeners.

Other Voices

*You cannot create experience.
You must undergo it.*
  ~ Albert Camus

OCTOBER

October 1

OUTAGES
...the shorter the better.

The storm raged for a while
before the power went out.
Then the rain slowed to a trickle
and I heard a thunderous clap
before the lights flickered off.

I thought to myself,
this could as easily be
an exploding transformer
as a bolt of lightning
darkening our block.
No matter which, I knew
it would likely be hours
before power was restored.

So what do you do
when the power goes out?

I went to bed,
tossed and turned,
took the dog out at 2 a.m.,
then got up at 6 a.m.
About that same time
the lights came back on.

Other Voices

Electricity is really just organized lightning.
~ George Carlin

October 2

LOVE IS
...who I am.

My father taught me
love is an angry, quiet man,
suffering in a deep silence
but steady as the day is long.

My mother taught me
love is what you do for others
by always saying yes
and sacrificing yourself.

My first wife taught me
love is a gaping hole
into which anyone can pour
the need to be needed.

This world taught me
love is a shiny mirror,
and the way to get love is
by earning enough to buy it.

Then darkness came,
bringing death along for a visit,
and through their sly counsel
I realized love is who I am.

Other Voices

*Truly, it is in darkness that one finds the light,
so when we are in sorrow,
then this light is nearest of all to us.*
~ MEISTER ECKHART

October 3

INTIMACY
...that deep longing within us all.

I am often reminded
prayer is a waking state.

God speaks to me
when I'm willing to listen,
as happened one evening in Texas
when a man named David
shared with our small group
that for him intimacy means
into-me-see.

I chuckled.
How cute and clever.
Still I had no idea
what he truly meant
until I learned to pray,
then began to see myself
in everyone and everything.

Everyone and everything,
even those way down
at the end of all roads,
are only longing to see
and to be seen.

Other Voices

*If fear is the great enemy of intimacy,
love is its true friend.*
~ Henri Nouwen

October 4

WE BELONG
Don't fight it.

We belong
right here,
right now.
Simply being
means something
nothingness
cannot comprehend.

Short or tall,
no matter
our gender,
our so-called race,
the religion
of our parents,
the persons
we may kiss,
how we talk,
the company
we choose to keep -

none of this matters
here, now,
anywhere, anytime
we can see
ourselves reflected
in the face of another.

Other Voices

*The essential dilemma of my life is between
my deep desire to belong and my suspicion of belonging.*
  ~ Jhumpa Lahiri

October 5

FOR ALL THOSE DAYS
Say it with me.

For all those days
requiring a strong drink
before they can be loosened
and then hastily taken off
like a restrictive tie or bra
or uncomfortable shoes.

For all those days
which spill into evenings
and are carried off to bed,
where they pollute our dreams
with acid-trippy visions
just real enough to frighten us
into questioning our sanity.

For all those days
that bleed into one another
in a long succession we call
same shit - different day,
but that eventually do give way
to the turning page
of season and sentiment,
thus revealing life anew.

Other Voices

It's ironic that in our culture everyone's biggest complaint is about not having enough time; yet nothing terrifies us more than the thought of eternity.
~ Dennis Miller

October 6

STARS ARE THE LIGHT
...to see into and beyond.

The ease and boredom
of a privileged life
makes any suffering
seem so much worse
than what we witness
in the suffering of those
with so much less.

Could it be because
we can now account
for the great many forces
moving heaven and earth,
and have given explanation
to everything demanding
to remain a mystery,
that our imagination withers
and we are unable to see
all suffering as one?

Other Voices

*Logic will get you from A to B.
Imagination will take you everywhere.*
~ Albert Einstein

October 7

BEATING HEART
The world is not machine!

Sometimes I don't realize
I'm doing what I'm doing,
or feeling what I'm feeling,
until I fall off to sleep,
trip down a rabbit hole
and reawaken to the subtle,
but no less profound reality
where everything speaks
and everything is connected
by fur, feather, feelings,
all as colors begin bleeding
into a beautiful, wet rainbow
right before abrupt re-entry
to my normal state -
a hyper-alertness clinging
to analytical understanding,
which always fails to explain
the subtext accompanying
my every action, conversation,
and the resultant emotions.

I write this to remember
the world is not machine.
It's a beating heart,
breathing lungs,
seeing eyes.

Other Voices

*In consequence of inventing machines,
men will be devoured by them.*
~ Jules Verne

October 8

FOOT RUB
with dog kisses

I protest
when she grabs my foot
and begins rubbing it
with that same hand
the dog was licking.

Hey!
she shoots back,
do you want me to stop?
The dog shows love by licking,
I'm just passing the love
on to you.

Other Voices
Dog is God spelled backwards.
~ ANONYMOUS

October 9

THIS SACRED SPACE
Don't just do something, sit there.

Quit looking for God.
God is already busy
looking for you.

And quit protesting.
It doesn't matter
if you're only seeking
a safe place to hide.

I know you,
because I am you.
I share your longing
for peace and serenity,
but know what we seek
often finds us first.

So let's call off our search,
recognizing this sacred space
is where we'll most likely find
God patiently waiting for us.

Other Voices

*Obsessed by a fairy tale,
we spend our lives searching for a magic door
and a lost kingdom of peace.*
~ Eugene O'Neill

October 10

MY FAVORITE COLORS
...are the words to this poem.

Here,
there,
everywhere,
I can see all
my favorite colors.

Light is broken and refracted.
Light is absorbed and reflected.
Light is ignited and extinguished.

Too much light
overwhelms color.
Too much dark
conceals color.

If you can find
just the right light,
the colors always
burst forth.

Other Voices

Nature always wears the colors of the spirit.
~ Ralph Waldo Emerson

October 11

A LOVE FEAST
...sustains our rapture.

The past is not a bone collector.
Rather, it's a giving spirit
who runs a lending library
containing your favorite songs,
along with the memories of when
you first heard those chords
and your heart leapt up to dance.

Abandon your past
and there will be nothing
for you to bring along,
into this present moment.

There will come a day
when you are invited to share
everything you stored away
at a great love feast.

Other Voices

Once I knew only darkness and stillness...
my life was without past or future...
but a little word from the fingers of another
fell into my hand that clutched at emptiness,
and my heart leaped to the rapture of living.
~ HELEN KELLER

October 12

OBLIVION
An ode to letting go of the past.

I can no longer ignore,
as I can no longer deny,
the soul-deep memories
connecting me to losses
now also lost to time.

There's a sound my soul makes
when remembering something
I thought long forgotten.

This great yowling halts
the hollowing out of my soul
by that radioactive dust
called forgetting.

My soul cannot forgive
and it cannot forget.
It must remember
to let go.

Other Voices

*The richness of life lies
in memories we have forgotten.*
~ Cesare Pavese

October 13

DECODING THE SPIRITS
Help me if you can.

The spirits must be confused,
they're speaking over each other.

This one says,
*Save nostalgia for after
the third glass of wine.*

That one says,
*Put your copper in a vault
but place your soul in a pocket
so you can spend it freely.*

Another chimes in,
*Visit the memories of your parents
until you know their story
better than your own.*

So here I sit,
a poet-messenger
with paper and ink,
yet without any idea
what all this means.

Help me if you can.
Read this poem twice
and allow these spirits
to have their say.

Other Voices

*A small body of determined spirits
fired by an unquenchable faith in their mission
can alter the course of history.*
~ Mahatma Gandhi

October 14

EVERYONE
...must trust their struggles.

I remind myself to be kind
because everyone walks
with an unseen limp.
Something big or small,
something physical
or psycho-spiritual,
slowing them down
on their difficult journey
to become exactly who
they are meant to be.

I say meant to be,
but maybe I could say
who they already are,
and remind them of how
they came into the world,
whole and unbroken,
not yet limping,
but also unaware the gifts
they bear along with them
are so longingly desired.

Other Voices

The old and honorable idea of 'vocation'
is simply that we each are called, by God,
or by our gifts, or by our preference,
to a kind of good work
for which we are particularly fitted.
~ WENDELL BERRY

October 15

A BETTER ME
...my lifelong task...

It's strange but true,
I've become a better me
through my failures
and my heartbreaks,
by thinking too much,
then refusing to let go,
by injury and infirmity
and by an imposed humility
which one day delivered me
to laughter and new friendships,
along with the strength
to be honest with myself,
no matter what the truth.

I've become a better me,
not by being the person
I thought I should be,
but by praying soulfully
to remember who I am,
and then allowing love
to change me.

Other Voices

*An arrogant person considers himself perfect.
This is the chief harm of arrogance.
It interferes with a person's main task in life -
becoming a better person.*
   ~ Leo Tolstoy

October 16

IMPERMANENCE
...is a guarantee.

Just because that rock
has sat on the ledge
for a million years
does not guarantee
it'll be there tomorrow.

And just because
people know your name
does not guarantee
you'll be remembered.

The hermit crab rents his shell
no longer than a day or two,
and the snake sheds her skin
when it's time for her to grow.
Yet we go into our homes
and quickly allow the walls
to harden all around us.

There is no unit of permanency
because there is no permanency.
We're all gifted a lifetime,
and likely the next time around
we'll be completely different.

Other Voices

*Your body is not who you are.
The mind and spirit transcend the body.*
~ Christopher Reeve

October 17

TIMELESS TRUTH
Forgive me the obvious.

I must remind myself often
there is no right way,
or else end up sacrificed
on the altar of perfection.

For the time being
I am done wandering.
I encountered my shadow
on overcrowded highways,
abandoned logging roads,
and in the mirror.

Now I can no longer care
whether I am judged harshly.
I try my best to see this world
through an open heart.

My soul is awakened
and reveals to me eternity
in the timeless movement
of great celestial bodies.

At long last I am free
to go about my business,
knowing God will use
my imperfect love
perfectly.

Other Voices

*You have your way. I have my way.
As for the right way, the correct way,
and the only way, it does not exist.*
~ FRIEDRICH NIETZSCHE

October 18

BIRKENSTOCK
An ode to gratitude.

Those sandals sitting there,
looking good for their age,
are now quite comfortable,
contoured perfectly to my feet.

I did not make them,
but wear them every day
regardless of the weather,
and without any worry
about my appearance.

Those sandals are a gift
from the sacrificial cow
who provided the leather,
from the skilled worker
who expertly sewed them,
from my mother who asked,
"What would you like
for your birthday?"

Other Voices

*When a person doesn't have gratitude,
something is missing in his or her humanity.*
~ Elie Wiesel

October 19

DID NOT LAST
An ode to equanimity.

There are sad days
when I recall friendships
that did not last,
yet had no ending,
no formal closure.

Yes, I know
that you too know
change is a constant,
and there is little peace
for those of us unable
to let go and live.

Still I want meaning,
a greater perspective
on the world I inhabit
and for the many lives
I touch and who touch me.

And I want to say
thank you, even though
our friendship did not last.

Other Voices

All the art of living lies in a fine mingling of letting go and holding on.
~ Havelock Ellis

October 20

INNER PEACE
It's always been there.

Today will be an easy day
if I can only let it be,
and not involve myself
in any great struggle
to make things right.

Gradually,
my days get easier
as I grow ever-softer
by reflecting on the ways
this world has shown me
love and tenderness.

A slow awakening,
a quiet meditation,
a walk in nature
all allow me to see
my world at peace.

Other Voices

*We are all on a journey
to mastering our inner peace.*
~ Raheem DeVaughn

October 21

WHO AM I KIDDING?
I never had a plan.

I no longer hold the illusion
my life will ever unfold
the way I thought it would.

Maybe it's because
so little has happened
I was told to expect,
I'm now ready to let go
of any certainty.

And it could be
that had my life gone
according to some plan,
it would've required me
to compromise my soul
and remain a child.

Other Voices

*To defer to someone else's definition
of a life well-lived is a Faustian bargain.*
~ RACHEL SIMMONS

October 22

OH, GROW UP!
It's not so bad.

Growing up is hard.
Of course, this is true.
But now I'm much older
and can say with certainty,
growing up means more
than years of struggle.

Among my fellow adults
I see too few prophets,
artists and leaders,
but plenty of adolescents
lacking any originality,
seeking only to conform.

I admit it's taken me
much too long to grow up,
and it may not have happened
without heartbreak and failure
and some necessary humility
forcing me to acknowledge
my own mortality.

Growing up means
growing down,
becoming rooted.

Growing up means
learning to become one
with life and death.

Growing up means
becoming awed
by the beauty of all life
in the radical quest
to transcend survival -

going beyond the known
until we are falling,
falling into the arms
of the creative force
called God.

Other Voices

*I hate that word, mature,
but I guess I am growing up.*
~ Sheryl Crow

October 23

WHAT AM I DOING?
A good question...

Yesterday I missed a meeting,
one I called and organized.
I'm sorry for wasting others' time,
but today take some satisfaction
at remembering my humanity.

Often I'm too busy
to connect the dots between
my doing and my being.
So forgetting a meeting,
missing phone calls,
or ignoring texts
snaps me out of hypnosis
and forces me into
a contemplative space
where I can ask myself:
What am I doing?

Other Voices

*Don't just do something,
sit there.*
~ Sylvia Boorstein

October 24

MEMORIES
Getting past the past...

What's now gone forever
you thought was safely
stored inside a box, put
where you'd remember it.

But gone, too, is all care,
once beyond any compare,
for the things in that box
you so longed to share.

Of course only God knows
the way each soul grows,
and everything in that box
was only a needless prop.

Other Voices

Memories are like mulligatawny soup in a cheap restaurant. It is best not to stir them.
 ~ P. G. WODEHOUSE

October 25

ADOPTION DAY
Gotta have faith...

Today we may adopt
another dog,
and so I'm sitting,
wondering:
*Who's more nervous,
me or that dog?*

For many years
I believed I knew exactly
what I needed and
how much I had
to give in return.

I was often wrong.

So today I step back
and pray that I will allow
kind spirits to show me
the way forward.

Other Voices

*Faith...
must be enforced by reason...
when faith becomes blind it dies.*
   ~ Mahatma Gandhi

HERE AND NOW
Where else?

You are who you are.
I am who I am.
There's no need
for us to become
anyone else.

The angels
waiting on the border
between here and there
warned me against
clinging to my life
as too precious,
or using death
as an easy excuse
for not showing up
to my life.

At my best
I am present
to who I truly am,
and also to who
others already are.

Other Voices

Don't cling to anything and don't reject anything.
  ~ HENEPOLA GUNARATANA

October 27

FIX EVERYTHING
Holding the tension with love...

This poem won't fix everything,
though the intention to fix
helps to move my pen.

A day like today,
after a difficult yesterday,
goes agonizingly slow,
in seconds and centimeters,
one deep breath to the next.

I feel sadness,
I feel regret.
I feel a bit lost,
yet can recognize
I acted with integrity,
spoke my truth,
and must now allow
the consequences
to find me.

I can see more clearly
at a great distance.
Therefore I wait patiently,
do and say little,
even when I witness
the struggling of others
and want to rescue them.

Other Voices

*I have just three things to teach:
simplicity, patience, compassion.
These three are your greatest treasures.*
~ Laozi

October 28

OTHER PEOPLE'S FEELINGS
Just listen.

Steer clear,
especially if you've got
the fix.

It's much better
not to go there.

Feelings are sticky
and you don't want
to handle them.

There's even a chance
you'll catch a fever
from the chill.

Really,
don't go there.

It's all headaches,
hot potatoes,
and broken glass.

Let me know
how it went.

Other Voices

*A person often meets his destiny
on the road he took to avoid it.*
~ Jean de La Fontaine

October 29

AS WATER GOES
...the soul goes.

I want you
and all the others
to like me.
I want my name
to sound sweet
when spoken,
to summon smiles
from its hearer.

By now we all know
if others think well of us
that just maybe we will
think better of ourselves.

Eventually
everything goes
as water goes -
falling wherever,
filling spaces,
finding gaps,
and evaporating
into thin air.

Time is our true need,
because it offers us
abundant opportunities
to get to know ourselves
in light and darkness,
for better and worse.

Time also plants a seed
deep inside the soul,
from which one day springs
a genuine self-acceptance.

Other Voices

The first step toward change is awareness.
The second step is acceptance.
  ~ Nathaniel Branden

October 30

DIVINE MYSTERY
...comes special delivery.

I had a plan for this poem,
along with some wise words
which seemed to have come
from another dimension
right into the thin air
I am breathing.

But that poem was not to be,
supplanted by this one
existing more in the milieu
of a day starting too early,
already fraught with worry.

*What could it be
which sets in motion
such negative thoughts?*

Now I hear a whisper
urging me to go with the flow,
and to receive divine mystery
as the very first delivery
of my waking day.

Other Voices

*Each time dawn appears,
the mystery is there in its entirety.*
~ René Daumal

October 31

GO AHEAD, CRY
Hear that lonesome whippoorwill...

If you're not going to cry,
go sit with the old men
slowly becoming a rock wall.

There's something to be said
for saying no
and for pushing back.

There's something to be admired
in knowing how
and in being certain.

And there's even something to
being the hammer
that gets the job done.

After all,
it's your stubborn resolve
that got you through
all the long, lonesome nights.

But now only tears
will keep you from hardening
into that rock wall.

Other Voices

*My entire soul is a cry,
and all my work is a commentary on that cry.*
~ Nikos Kazantzakis

NOVEMBER

November 1

HERE ALL ALONG
...in the presence of eternity...

This is another poem,
not about the poem
I planned to write,
but about the one
still being written.

My mind is full of ideas,
but my soul works
antithetically.

Wouldn't you agree
our experiences take root,
fed by our emotions
flooding inward?

Yet who we truly are
is never the person
we come to know
through all that heavy
thinking and feeling.

The chaos and hellfire
we once invited
in the sincere desire
to know our souls,
becomes tiresome
as we grow older,
less romantic.

When every other thing
slows down to a trickle,
we find who we really are
was here all along.

Other Voices

No, I never saw an angel,
but it is irrelevant whether I saw one or not.
I feel their presence around me.
   ~ Paul Coelho

November 2

PULL THE PLUG
Empty yourself.

Slowly
pour,
exhale
and release
the stores
of emotion
written
in the ways
you carry
life's lessons.

You're holding
so much more
than a mirror
will show you.

Call
to your soul.

Ask
to be shown
the drain
through which
you may empty
yourself.

Other Voices

Hell is empty and all the devils are here.
~ WILLIAM SHAKESPEARE

November 3

BEFORE I BEGIN...
I'm thinking of the way dogs touch noses.

I hope you're feeling vulnerable,
and that we're drawn together
by our vulnerability.

It's not always how we meet,
but what we bring with us
that creates the sacred space
in which we may know God.

Yet if at this very moment
our hearts resist love's calling,
let's seek counsel from the mystics
and be open to their wisdom.

Other Voices

Each day holds a surprise.
But only if we expect it can we see,
hear, or feel it when it comes to us.
Let's not be afraid to receive each day's surprise,
whether it comes to us as sorrow or as joy.
It will open a new place in our hearts,
a place where we can welcome new friends
and celebrate more fully our shared humanity.
~ Henri Nouwen

November 4

SO SIMPLE
...like apple pie.

It's as simple as sidewalks
and making eye contact,
as simple as saying hello
and holding the door.

It's as simple as letting go
and then doing less,
as simple as breathing
and smiling more.

It's as simple as it is
when life is no longer
simply about survival,
but sharing your love.

Other Voices

*We shall never know all the good
that a simple smile can do.*
~ Mother Teresa

November 5

GUY FAWKES
Remember, remember!

The fifth of November...
My Guy Fawkes mask
is now but a memory,
left behind to that Halloween
when a guard warned me,
*You can't bring
that into the stadium.*

I miss that mask,
with its thick brows
and wide, smug grin.
It makes those comfortable
within the status quo
a little bit uneasy.

It even makes those
sympathetic to the suffering
a little uneasy.

Other Voices

Remember, remember!
The fifth of November,
The Gunpowder treason and plot;
I know of no reason
Why the Gunpowder treason
Should ever be forgot!
Guy Fawkes and his companions
Did the scheme contrive,
To blow the King and Parliament
All up alive.
Threescore barrels, laid below,
To prove old England's overthrow.
But, by God's providence, him they catch,
With a dark lantern, lighting a match!
A stick and a stake
For King James's sake!
If you won't give me one,
I'll take two,
The better for me,
And the worse for you.
A rope, a rope, to hang the Pope,
A penn'orth of cheese to choke him,
A pint of beer to wash it down,
And a jolly good fire to burn him.
Holloa, boys! holloa, boys! make the bells ring!
Holloa, boys! holloa boys! God save the King!
Hip, hip, hooor-r-r-ray!
~ ENGLISH FOLK VERSE

November 6

SOURCE TO MOUTH
Oh, great river!

    Rio Grande,
    great river!
    Rio Grande,
    great river!

    You flow
    downstream,
    always downstream,
    so easy,
    easy and winding,
    never worried
    about picking up,
    then depositing
    leaf, stone, bodies.

    Rio Grande,
    great river!

    So goes my journey,
    beginning at its source
    deep within my soul,
    slowly winding its way
    through my body,
    picking up and dropping off
    blood, bile, bone,
    spilling out of my mouth
    with the words
    I love you.

Other Voices

*If you have a river,
then you should share it with everyone.*
   ~ CHEN GUANGBIAO

November 7

GREAT CONVERSATIONS
...are about learning to love.

Most mornings
you may find me here,
quietly praying for the fog
to fall away from my gaze.

Slowly,
trees, rivers
and mountains
come into focus,
along with birds,
busy squirrels,
and tiny bugs.

It seems I alone
observe this scene
with any distance,
any sense of self.

Timidly,
I begin to speak:

*Oh, Great River,
Oh, Great Mountain,
Oh, Wise Tree,
teach me the song
the birds are now singing.*

I commune here
so that I too may learn
to love with abandon.

Other Voices

*You won't fight to save
what you haven't learned to love.*
~ Belden Lane

November 8

OVERCOME
...by my life.

Everything
and all at once.
This is how my life
rushes towards me:
Hot in the summer,
cold in the winter,
wet in the rain,
frightening at night.

If sometimes
I'm not overcome
and overwhelmed
by living my life,
something is wrong.

And if I'm not awed
each time I pause
to admire the distance
you, me, and everyone
has traveled to be right here,
it's probably time for me
to double my pace.

Other Voices

*A man who has not passed
through the inferno of his passions
has never overcome them.*
~ CARL JUNG

November 9

A BIGGER FIGHT
...is not inevitable.

Here come familiar feelings.
Fear and anxiety are on the march,
but I refuse to meet them head-on.
Force creates a counter-force.

So I let them pass.
Maybe they'll detain me,
take me away to a dark room
and show me all the things
I'd rather not see.

But if I don't resist
they soon grow weary,
then quickly head off
seeking a bigger fight.

Other Voices

*The supreme art of war
is to subdue the enemy without fighting.*
～ SUN TZU

November 10

IT'S NOT TIME
...yet.

It's cold,
too damn cold.
Only a few days ago
I was burnin' up
in the late season sun.

Warm in my office,
I feel open to suggestion
as I try finding cracks
in the absolute certainty
wanting to claim me,
both body and soul,
for the machine world.

So I ask the maple trees
right outside my window,
Why do you hold tightly
to your leaves?

The wind swells,
gathering in their branches.
Then I hear them reply,
Soon, but now's not time
to let them all go.

Other Voices

It is easier to find men who will volunteer to die,
than to find those who are willing to endure pain with patience.
~ Julius Caesar

November 11

CALL TO YOUR SOUL
It may come running.

Call to your soul
and it may come running.

Call to your soul
and it may come running.

Call to your soul
and it may come running.

Why won't you
call to your soul?

Other Voices

Everything is soul and flowering.
  ~ Rumi

November 12

SECOND SPRING
...amidst the fallen leaves...

All the leaves are brown
and have fallen to the ground
beneath the young ash tree
anchored to the hill beside me.

While I rake those leaves
my thoughts turn to music,
some sort of distraction
from the cold and my chore.

I want rhythm and rhyme,
a quick turn of phrase,
and a driving, energetic beat
to keep me warm until I finish.

But my soul desires country music,
simple words and string instruments.
It wants to be told a good story,
and for me to let the leaves lie.

Other Voices

*Autumn is a second spring
when every leaf is a flower.*
~ ALBERT CAMUS

November 13

FOLD 'EM
...but find an ace you can keep.

I'm a lousy poker player,
always tipping my hand,
unable to keep a straight face
while holding only two pair.

But it doesn't matter anymore.
My soul has been nagging me
to stop worrying about winning,
to go out and invite everyone else
not already sitting at the big table
to take a seat and learn the game.

Life has dealt me many good hands
I've had the choice to play or fold,
but now my only real option
is to put down the cards
and learn how to love.

Other Voices

I'm not like a poker player. I'm not into bluff.
My way is to look someone in the eye
and tell them the way I'm intending to go.
My cards are always on the table.
   ~ Tori Amos

November 14

A SLAVE SHIP CALLED JESUS*
Have you heard the joke

*about the Holocaust Survivor,
who died of old age and
came upon God in Heaven?*

*He decided to tell God
a joke about the Holocaust.
God replied, "That isn't funny."
To which the survivor responded,
"I guess you had to be there."
...*

Those cynical jokes,
at which I laugh the most,
reveal something about me,
something I'd rather not see
or haven't been able to see.

My beef with God
was always paper thin,
never carrying the weight
of existential betrayal
like the kind wrought
by holocaust, slavery,
or nightmarish trauma.

For me, God was irreconcilable
with the rational world I knew,
until I encountered a darkness
for which there was no answer.

Only then
I realized how limited
was the God I understood,
and how unlimited divine love is

in creating a world far beyond
my limited comprehension.

*Jesus of Lübeck

Other Voices

Si comprehendis, non est Deus.
If you comprehend, it is not God.
~ Augustine of Hippo

November 15

MUSICAL CHAIRS
...like an endless merry-go-round.

The game musical chairs
still fills me with anxiety,
just as it did forty years ago
when I first learned to play.

There's always one less chair
than there are people playing.
Round and round everyone goes
until the music stops suddenly,
leaving that chairless person
dejected, standing alone.

Today it seems as though
I'm still playing this game,
clawing and fighting through life
so that I won't be the one
left without a seat.

Will this game ever end?
Must the music go on forever?
Or must I find the courage within
to walk away and face my fears?

Other Voices

*The whole aim of practical politics
is to keep the populace alarmed
(and hence clamorous to be led to safety)
by menacing it with an endless series of hobgoblins,
all of them imaginary.*
~ H. L. MENCKEN

November 16

ALWAYS REMEMBER
...to the Earth you belong.

River says,
cry me
into existence.

Tree says,
stand tall
and go deep.

Mountain says,
rise up
and be broken down.

Sun says,
burn, baby, burn
all day long.

Moon says,
sleep, child, sleep,
the sun's done gone.

Little bird says,
be happy,
sing a love song.

Worm says,
always remember,
to the Earth you belong.

Other Voices

Let the rain kiss you.
Let the rain beat upon your head
with silver liquid drops.
Let the rain sing you a lullaby.
    ~ Langston Hughes

November 17

CONFORMITY
...is killing us.

It's not quite the same
as going along to get along.
Rather, it's going along
to get our just desserts.

I can't possibly be
the only one struggling
to stay in lockstep with
this ridiculous beat.

Have you asked yourself,
why do I do what I do,
and is it even worth doing?

Aren't we all drawn
toward the oddballs?
We can't help but notice
they don't quite fit in.

Maybe they secretly wish
to be like everyone else.
But wouldn't we rather be free
from our burden to conform?

Other Voices

Conformity is the jailer of freedom and the enemy of growth.
~ JOHN F. KENNEDY

November 18

FOR WHAT IT'S WORTH
What's worth remembering, and then forgetting?

You say your demented mother
no longer remembers your father,
yet you notice how her face softens
when she hears stories about him.

Every day you drive to work
on a road called Victory Parkway.
But no one seems to remember
the victory it commemorates.

You usually recall
names you need to know,
where you left your keys,
significant dates,
what others will forget,
a childhood wound,
your favorite recipe,
the steep price you paid
to get where you are.

Some will call you lucky
if you can let go and forget
all of the worthless things,
especially your resentments.

But rest assured, knowing
there are also as many things
well worth remembering
as there are to forget.

Other Voices

*A sorrow's crown of sorrow
is remembering happier times.*
~ Alfred, Lord Tennyson

November 19

ROCK IN MY SHOE
How the hell did it get there?

Sometimes there comes
a long moment of serenity,
when I can look around,
and upon exhaling notice,
nothing remains undone,
and thus there is absolutely
nothing else for me to do.

The more tightly I cling
to my own understanding,
the less truth it holds
in this world of forms
animated by the formless.

I love those long moments
when my life slips out of focus
and there is no firm context
to distract my understanding.

Everything is essential,
even the rock in my shoe,
though I have no idea
how it got there.

Other Voices

*The precision of naming takes away
from the uniqueness of seeing.*
~ Pierre Bonnard

November 20

LITTLE ME
...does plenty.

Nothing needing doing
ever remains undone.

I'm not held responsible
for the rising of the sun.
It's not me who commands
the tide or the wind.
And I cannot wake
the trees in the spring.

All I can be
is little me,
not too big or insignificant,
free-floating
amidst all things
seen and unseen.

With each breath
I do what's mine to do,
and somehow my soul
is unified in creation.

Other Voices

*Little things seem nothing,
but they give peace,
like those meadow flowers
which individually seem odorless
but all together perfume the air.*
~ Georges Bernanos

November 21

WINTER WEATHER
...returns.

This early season snow
falls like a heavy hand
upon my shoulder,
urging me to slow down.

Somewhere it's sunny,
and a warm breeze
stirs up energy
in all the busy people.

Here the Earth sleeps
and a cold wind
slows the breath
in all the drowsy people.

Other Voices

*The woods are lovely, dark and deep.
But I have promises to keep,
and miles to go before I sleep.*
  ~ Robert Frost

November 22

THE FIXERS
It's good to know at least one.

It's an ordinary night
and here we're gathered,
a bunch of misfits
middle-aged and older,
sitting around a table
in the windowless basement
of a downtown church.

Everyone wants to help,
and everyone is just a little bit
too helpful and too knowledgeable.
That's how we came to be here,
this community of fixers.

What else is there to say?
It's just an ordinary night
and the fixers are gathered
to do what we do.

Other Voices

*I try to be the fixer of situations
and I gravitate to people who are institutional misfits.*
~ Stephan Jenkins

November 23

A GREAT AWAKENING
You'll know it by its love.

This only just occurred to me,
though it seems like an old truth:
*We create the world we fear
because fear tells us it's inevitable.*

We can consult sages and mystics,
but we need only to look into a mirror
to see violence begets violence,
while love generates even more love.

Few are born truly alive.
More are jolted awake by living.
Yet most of us will still need others
to offer us a gentle patience,
and to point to those deeper truths,
which at first seem contradictory
or as cute riddles to be solved.

*Have you ever seen a great awakening?
Would you even know it if you had?*

I think it might be frightening
and accompanied by terrible suffering,
before calming into the peacefulness
of a transcendent acceptance
at the dawning of a new day.

Other Voices

That is the real spiritual awakening, when something emerges from within you that is deeper than who you thought you were. So, the person is still there, but one could almost say that something more powerful shines through the person.
~ Eckhart Tolle

November 24

SACRED REASONS
...are many.

My heart says,
Let's get little.
Let's talk about something
meaningful in this moment.

Yes,
I reply,
let's do this!

So last night
I had a conversation
I'll call *Sacred Reasons.*

My host said he quit smoking
and it wasn't at all difficult,
he only needed a reason.

And there I sat,
holding his reason,
a beautiful baby girl.

Now I can think of nothing else
but all of the sacred reasons,
grounding us in our being
and calling forth our love.

Other Voices

The road to the sacred leads through the secular.
~ Abraham Joshua Heschel

November 25

BAKED
...into bread for others.

Everyday I must resist
the hardening happening
in this large oven
I call my life.

Things happen for good reason.
Things happen for no reason.
Regardless, I can count on time
to dispel my convictions.

When it's sunny I look into water
to see myself and the blue sky.
When it's cloudy I look into water
to see what's swimming beneath.

Today I pray to be baked,
but only to a soft perfection,
so I may then become
like bread for others,
palatable and life-affirming.

Other Voices

*Peace goes into the making of a poem
as flour goes into the making of bread.*
~ PABLO NERUDA

November 26

NUMB
Don't worry everything's just fine.

It kinda feels like cheating
to sit and write a poem
right after visiting a place
where the spirits can roam free;
a space where breath and time
cease to be of any concern.

But now I'm walking the streets
in the company of troubled people,
forgetting I am one of them.

I hear a man saying,
*I'm just trying to change
how it is I'm feeling.
I want to be numb.*

When I leave the city
for a week, a day, an hour,
or just one minute,
upon returning
I, too, want to go numb.

Presence isn't about
climbing a mountain
to watch the eagles soar.
It's about going somewhere
I don't ever want to go,
and keeping company
with those who disturb me,
while doing what's mine to do
in the mud of living poetry.

Other Voices

*When you're in survival mode,
you numb yourself.*
~ Clemantine Wamariya

November 27

CULTS
...are everywhere.

We live in a cult called *country*.
We often gather in cults
at sporting events and churches.
Families are still smaller cults,
and our rituals and addictions,
especially those shrouded in secrecy,
have become the cult of self.

A childish understanding of cults
goes no further than secret societies,
and mysterious zealots in long robes
stealing away to meet by firelight.

Of course not all cults are bad.
Many may serve a good purpose.
But like other human constructs,
cults are no more permanent
than rain falling in the desert,
and can offer us little insight
into the true nature of belonging.

Other Voices

The figure a poem makes. It begins in delight and ends in wisdom... in a clarification of life - not necessarily a great clarification, such as sects and cults are founded on, but in a momentary stay against confusion.
~ ROBERT FROST

November 28

RECKLESSNESS
There's an inevitability to it.

This is what I do now -
sit and listen to my soul.

There's no one in the dark
holding a blade to my throat.
I don't need sharp objects
to puncture the underbelly
containing my being.

I'm already bleeding.
Can't you tell?

Life flows out of me
on to this page
and all over my work,
which no longer is
the thing I want to do,
but rather the very thing
my soul bids me to do.

I once thought
without words I am nothing.
Now I know absolutely
there aren't enough words,
not enough sounds,
to describe this life.

So why do I bother writing?
In such recklessness
I come alive.

Other Voices

Why should we honour those that die upon the field of battle?
A man may show as reckless a courage
in entering into the abyss of himself.
~ WILLIAM BUTLER YEATS

November 29

RELAX
...and quit trying so hard.

Those of us who wander too far
soon learn you'll only get lost.
And those of us who climb and climb
will learn you never reach the top.

I'm so often reminded
there's absolutely nothing
God needs to be done,
that I alone must do.

When I lean into the wind
I can hear thousands of voices
all buzzing in unison,
Quit trying so hard!

Other Voices

*Some people are so heavenly minded
that they are no earthly good.*
~ Oliver Wendell Holmes, Sr.

November 30

RESPONSIBILITY
...sits where I sit.

My father taught me
my life is about responsibility,
a commitment unto death.

Now you know why
I'm always so serious,
and not one of those poets
who revels in drunkenness
while dancing at Carnival
in the streets of Rio.

I've tried and tried,
but could never get
far enough away from
the very real burden
of my responsibilities.

Here where I am
my responsibility sits,
not having moved an inch
since I was ten years old.
Like my breath it grows
then shrinks in size.
I try to make peace with it
by becoming softer.

Other Voices

You cannot escape the responsibility of tomorrow by evading it today.
~ Abraham Lincoln

DECEMBER

December 1

NO SIGNAL
...no stirring songs

The radio I use
to listen to my soul-songs
isn't working.

It must be because the silence
isn't broadcasting this morning.
Thus I won't be able to tune
the receiver I keep in my heart
to a signal my head can amplify.

All I feel is the cold pushing
inward through these walls
while I listen to the hum
of the space heater pushing back.

It's one of those mornings,
nondescript and not urgent,
just waiting with ambivalence
for me to shake things up.

Other Voices

Wise men speak because they have something to say;
Fools because they have to say something.
   ~ Plato

December 2

SOUL TALK
It's all true.

Cut off your head.
You won't need it
to locate your heart,
asleep near the center
of your animate being.

Yet don't lose your head.
Store it somewhere safe.
You may still need it
to set all the clocks
and predict the weather.

But for now,
listen to my voice.
I am your soul,
unique and subversive,
a non-native speaker.

For years you treated me
like an unstable child.
Have you forgotten
when we played together?

It's time to come out
as who you truly are,
headless and humble,
heart open to receive.

Other Voices

*Inasmuch as love grows in you,
insomuch beauty grows;
for love is itself the beauty of the soul.*
~ AUGUSTINE OF HIPPO

December 3

TICK OF THE CLOCK
Tick...Tock...Tick...Tock

Some can hear
the ticking of the clock.
I can feel it -
tick, tock,
tick, tock.

My heart beats
to the rhythm of that clock,
twisting and turning
inside my head.

Tick,
I grow weary
of my unending lust.

Tock,
I am jaded
by my dead living.

Then from the dark
comes a voice offering
to silence that clock.

It tolls a chime of belonging
and whispers to me:

*Hear what you hear,
and see what you see.
Accept yourself, then become
who you're meant to be.*

Other Voices

*The hours of folly are measured by the clock;
but of wisdom, no clock can measure.*
~ WILLIAM BLAKE

December 4

THE APPALACHIANS
Listen when they speak.

When the mountains speak
all I hear is forever talk
about molten fire,
strange creatures,
endless flora,
swirling west winds,
and the shrugging off
of glacial overcoats.

These mountains are gentle,
broken and calmed by the eons,
and now welcoming to us all.
The trees know them better,
sinking their roots deep below
the rolling surface of their ridges.

The mighty oak tells me,
*We're all just another epoch
in the life of a mountain.*

Other Voices

*My father considered a walk among the mountains
as the equivalent of churchgoing.*
~ Aldous Huxley

December 5

MAYBE
...and probably

Maybe the fog is hiding something
the dawn doesn't want us to see.

Maybe the bees don't care
for the smell of dandelions.

Maybe the roads joke to each other
about seeming to lead nowhere.

Maybe the moon laughs hysterically
when the sea complains of tired feet.

Maybe a mirror reflects only
what we are expecting to see.

And maybe God is the only one
who can hold all perspectives.

Other Voices

*Maybe Christmas, the Grinch thought,
doesn't come from a store.*
～ Dr. Seuss

December 6

AT HOME
...is where love begins.

Not since I was a child
have I felt that profound sense
of love and of being right at home,
nor now being so long removed,
felt such a longing to get it back.

The sentiment I call home
must at times ebb and flow,
as I journey through my life
and at various stages need
the grounding that comes
from a place to call home.

When I can trust
all is exactly as it should be,
then there is no place on Earth
I will not be at home.

Other Voices

Where thou art, that is home.
~ EMILY DICKINSON

December 7

A DAY OFF
Have you ever wondered...

What might happen
if you took a day off,
did nothing,
went nowhere,
and spoke to no one?

Would you lose your job?
Would you starve?
Would your family suffer?
Would you begin to remember
what you've tried to forget?
Would you become empty
and lose yourself?
Would anyone stop loving you?
Would you slowly disappear,
along with all meaning
that comes from your doing?
Would the world end?

So why is it
your soul keeps asking you
to take a day off?

Other Voices

*We had a day off here yesterday
and I just sat in my room and played.*
~ Leo Kottke

December 8

BRIAN SHRUGGED
…and so would John Galt.

Have you ever seen
an image of the mighty Atlas
bravely shouldering this world?

I always doubted Atlas
because I couldn't determine
what ground he was standing on,
though clever folks assured me,
"It's turtles all the way down."

This world,
on top of Atlas,
on top of a turtle,
on top of a turtle,
on down…

Because I wouldn't build my life
on such a rickety structure,
I took up the weight of the world,
trying to bear the responsibility
upon my mortal shoulders.

But you know how the story goes.

It turned out to be much more
than I alone could bear,
the needless headaches
and inevitable heartaches.

Now I'm quite content
to leave the weight of this world
to Atlas, the turtles, and God
- just so long as I alone
don't have to shoulder it.

Other Voices

*Drop the idea that you are Atlas
carrying the world on your shoulders.
The world would go on even without you.
Don't take yourself so seriously.*
  ~ Norman Vincent Peale

December 9

ONE AND THE SAME
...like night and day.

Whatever I offer this world
is returned to me this morning
in resounding claps of thunder
and bursts of fiery lightning
right outside my window.

I welcome the wind.
I bless the rain.
Water eventually comes
to those who are thirsty.

It's from stillness
the wind begins to blow,
and then back into stillness
where the wind goes to rest.

The wet and the dry,
the quiet and the loud,
the strong and the weak,
the painful and pleasurable,
are all from the same source.

Other Voices

I have two pairs of reading glasses.
One pair is for reading fiction,
the other for non-fiction.
I've read the Bible twice wearing each pair,
and it's the same.
   ~ STEVEN WRIGHT

December 10

WE'RE ALL POETS
...moonlighting by day.

We're all poets.
You and I know this.
Some of us use words,
others a handful of notes,
and still others
beautiful movements.

Have you met the poet making coffee?
Or the one driving for Uber?
Maybe your poet pours beer,
then listens to how your day went.

There is no better medicine
for the long, sleepless nights,
and for learning to let go,
than the ways we embody poetry
so our souls may be set free.

Other Voices

*If you want poets in space,
you'll have to wait.*
    ~ Buzz Aldrin

December 11

TRUSTING UNCERTAINTY
...is the cornerstone of faith.

>Strange dreams lead
>to an unsettled awakening,
>and to feeling stranded
>far from my home.
>
>Everything seems normal
>as I go about my daily routine
>in familiar surroundings.
>Yet I cannot find within
>safe ground to rest upon.
>
>This is when age-old spirits
>are called into service.
>They whisper into my ear,
>*Trust the uncertainty.*
>*You can trust the uncertainty.*

Other Voices

>*All I have seen teaches me to trust the creator*
>*for all I have not seen.*
>~ Ralph Waldo Emerson

December 12

LOST IN PRESIDIO
...but found by the desert.

Several years ago,
if you were in Presidio, Texas
on a dusty day in May,
we might've had lunch together
at a busy Mexican restaurant.

You probably noticed my blue car
and wondered how an Ohioan
had wandered so far from home.

And I probably did nothing
to hide the fact that I was lost
and glad to find a place to eat.

Could you tell it was my birthday?
And did you order the chicken mole?
I remember how good it tasted,
but doubt I'll ever go back for more.

Other Voices

*If you ever find happiness by hunting for it,
you will find it, as the old woman did her lost spectacles,
safe on her own nose all the time.*
  ~ Josh Billings

December 13

LISTEN FROM THE HEART
It's the best way to hear.

Listen from the heart.
The heart has ears
but no head to judge
the words it is hearing.

Listen from the heart.
Let it bleed for you
as your soul struggles
to find its voice.

Listen from the heart.
Let it reveal the limits
of thinking and knowing
in an infinite universe.

Listen from the heart.
Let the heart be your hands
with which you reach out
to embrace everything.

Other Voices

*Somewhere we know that without silence
words lose their meaning,
that without listening
speaking no longer heals,
that without distance
closeness cannot cure.*
~ HENRI NOUWEN

December 14

SPEAK FROM THE HEART
It's the best way to share.

Speak from the heart.
The heart knows best
how to describe lovingly
what your head is thinking.

Speak from the heart.
The heart knows instinctively
how to express with tenderness
what your gut is feeling.

Speak from the heart.
The heart knows intuitively
how to convey your desire
for soulful intimacy.

Speak from the heart.
The heart sees others fully,
and will allow them to speak
through their own tender hearts.

Other Voices

*Before the tongue can speak,
it must have lost the power to wound.*
~ Peace Pilgrim

December 15

BE SPONTANEOUS AND AUTHENTIC
No problem.

If you cannot stay awake
to see the full moon,
get up a little early
and watch it go down.

Allow the distinct seasons
to delight you with colors,
and the rivers to show you
how to move through life.

Grow in love mysteriously,
even when you are troubled
by the limitations of your love
in finding a higher ground.

Take pains to be patient.
Take time for pleasure.
Take nothing for granted.
Be spontaneous and authentic.

Other Voices

The essence of pleasure is spontaneity.
~ GERMAINE GREER

December 16

BE LEAN OF EXPRESSION
...to strengthen your authority.

    Shout into the silence
    and it will eat your words.
    Tear the solitude with your screams
    and it well sew serenity anew.

    Think back to a moment
    when someone truly heard you.
    Were you even speaking?

    Don't offer too many words,
    especially those carrying no weight.
    Speak only if the spirit moves you
    and be lean of expression.

    Someone wise once said,
    Preach the Gospel at all times,
    and use words if you must.

Other Voices

Music is the silence between the notes.
~ Claude Debussy

December 17

TILT TENDERLY
...as tenderness is a virtue.

Tilt tenderly,
listening, holding,
waiting patiently
for love to reach up,
snatch you by the collar,
and then pull you down
to the ground of your being.

Tilt tenderly your stoic heart
toward the innocent and the dying.
They hear music and dance easily
while you stand rigid, making excuses.

Tilt tenderly your rational mind
toward the absurdities of life,
like pain without reason
and God's unconditional love.

Tilt tenderly toward solidarity.
Tilt tenderly toward solitude.
Tilt tenderly toward silence.
Tilt tenderly toward singing.
Tilt tenderly toward that something
already tilting tenderly toward you.

Other Voices

There is no charm equal to tenderness of heart.
~ Jane Austen

December 18

REST ASSURED
...you are not God.

Most of us never rest
until we have arrived
at the limit of our control,
gone beyond the boundaries
of our finite understanding,
and felt the terrible pain
of letting go.

*But, oh, how sweet it is
to awaken powerless!*

What freedom it allows
for us to become human,
that being our soul desires,
reborn just the right size
to do what is ours to do.

Rest assured,
you are not God.

Other Voices

Let go and let God...
~ Twelve Step Wisdom

December 19

SOME REASON
There's gotta be one.

There must be some reason
for all the things I know,
and even better reasons
for what I don't.

Some days I feel punch drunk,
all the contents of my mind spilled
out on the table of conversation
but not food enough to feed anyone.

So here I am,
twisting and turning,
unable to find comfort,
while sitting in my easy chair
as it tosses and turns like a tiny boat
adrift in a sea of uncertainty.

Above the water
I see the clouds and the sky.

Under the water
my thoughts go down deep
to what's nibbling at my toes.

There must be some reason
I woke today in cloud-cuckoo-land.

There must also be some reason
I can never say what I mean perfectly.

And there must be some reason
we're all here in this place,
trying to figure it out together.

Other Voices

*Reason has always existed,
but not always in a reasonable form.*
~ KARL MARX

December 20

REMEMBERING
...the best that we can.

Memory is a hole,
but not simply a void
where the truth is twisted
or forgotten altogether.

I'm thinking more
along the lines of the hole
Alice entered to dine
at the Mad Hatter's table.

And I've never seen a photo
that can tell a story more faithfully
than an earnest account given
by the bearer of a faulty memory.

We all try our best to remember
what it's important not to forget,
so that we may live more wholly
within the never-ending present.

Other Voices

*Memory is a complicated thing,
a relative to truth,
but not its twin.*

~ Barbara Kingsolver

December 21

FIRE AND ICE
...brings the soul alive.

Come to me hot.
Come to me cold.
But if you are tepid,
don't come at all.

I want your fire and ice,
not platitudes and half-truths
diced with apples and cinnamon,
baked into the American Dream.

Life is lived in fire and ice.
Everyone baptized by heartache
knows this as the gospel truth.

From the fiery chaos of relationship,
to the icy wilderness of loneliness,
God is stirring us in one great pot.

Take the education.
Take the spouse.
Take the job.
Take the house.
Take the money.
Take retirement, too.
Take whatever the middle gives you,
but for the soul it just won't do.

Other Voices

*Move into the emptiness
of question and answer and question.*
   ~ Rumi

December 22

DRIFTING
...in and out.

I made it through the night
hour by creeping hour.
My bedroom clock is digital
and therefore has no tick-tock
to hypnotize me back to sleep.

So I lay there counting,
first backwards from 100,
and then the shrinking minutes
before I must face a new day.

Eventually I heard a gentle voice
trying to calm me back to sleep.

Why do you worry so much?
Live each day as it comes
and rest assured all is well.
Trust that you will heal,
and thus inspire others
in their own healing.

All my other sleepless nights
have taught me not to argue,
but to thank that gentle voice
and to accept life's blessings,
even if I can't get back to sleep.

Other Voices

I love sleep.
My life has the tendency
to fall apart when I'm awake,
you know?
~ Ernest Hemingway

December 23

IMMORTALITY
What's the point?

The immortals must be bored.
They've got nothing much to do,
even though they have plenty of time
and can do anything they want.

I've always wondered
whether immortals really exist
or if I might just be consumed
by my own mortality.

Others assure me I've lived before,
agreeing just prior to my birth
to forget everything I once knew
and to return in innocence.

Accepting my life will one day end
and uncertain whether I'll be back,
I probably ought to get busy.
I have so much yet to learn.

Other Voices

*One has to pay dearly for immortality;
one has to die several times while one is still alive.*
~ Friedrich Nietzsche

December 24

BORN AGAIN
A prayer to forget myself.

Tell the wind
I'm done resisting.
Tell the rain,
and the steep path, too.

At last I'm grateful to surrender,
allowing the current to push me
anywhere I wouldn't voluntarily go.

I've been piloting my life for years
but now find this task a burden.
Because I succeeded in becoming me,
it's time to grow into something more.

Warrior, Lover, Magician,
King and Queen -
these roles aren't meant
to last our lifetime.

Thus I'm slowly removing
this heavy mantle I've been wearing.

Today I call myself poet,
which speaks not of my certainty,
but of my spirit kinship
with the wind and rolling hills.

Other Voices

Throw your dreams into space like a kite,
and you do not know what it will bring back,
a new life, a new friend, a new love, a new country.
   ~ ANAÏS NIN

December 25

YEAR END
A strange Christmas Poem.

At last it arrives,
whatever you've been expecting,
what you said you really wanted
alongside what you don't want
from any unavoidable surprise.

The holidays may be delivered
neatly wrapped in pretty paper,
but they often visit with company
in the form of mild disappointment
that can linger during a long week
lasting from Monday 'till Sunday.

O, 'tis true!
Somewhere it's summertime,
but first you must endure
this damn winter weather
with no remedy until spring.

Try to persevere,
knowing this long season
is often followed by good news,
coming on the last day of the month,
during the wee hours of night,
at the tolling of the clock.

Other Voices

*Happy, happy Christmas, that can win us back
to the delusions of our childhood days,
recall to the old man the pleasures of his youth,
and transport the traveler back to his own fireside and quiet home!*
  ~ CHARLES DICKENS

December 26

A BLESSING
...in this present moment.

At times it frightens me
how quickly I lose my faith.
But then it comes rushing back
in the notes of a beloved song
I know I won't ever forget.

Often, it's something in the moment
that sends me headlong into tomorrow,
a magical place where I expect freedom
from all those things I worry about.

The problem with living in the future
is that it quickly enslaves today,
snatching away this present moment
before I can experience it fully
and know its true blessing.

Other Voices

*You must live in the present,
launch yourself on every wave,
find your eternity in each moment.*
  ~ Henry David Thoreau

December 27

FALLING WATER
...is washing over me.

Whenever I tell the story
of who I think I am,
my first task is always
to dig into the past
or gaze into the future
for the smart words
my ego would approve.

They sound like this:

*I am from here,
by way of these people,
and grew up doing
what made me who I am.*

*And if I could divine
the future of my life
I am certain I would have it made,
because of all those difficult things
I've faced until this day.*

But it no longer matters
if my words can persuade.
I know my life is only
falling water,
washing over me.

Other Voices

*If you've heard this story before,
don't stop me,
because I'd like to hear it again.*
~ Groucho Marx

December 28

PEACE NOW
...in this fire.

It's always something.
Isn't it?

I mean the moments are few
when nothing's happening,
when nothing's changing,
and there's nothing to worry about.

Someone please remind me
to relish all the boring days,
even though it may become
easy to lose my sense of God
in the sameness.

Peace is
the increasingly rare gift
of monotonous and empty time,
- time to watch the sun rise
and watch the grass grow
before the sun sets.

If there's only one thing
bringing me closer to the stillness
and to the peace now in this fire,
it's my growing understanding of a God
much bigger than I ever imagined.

Other Voices

The cost of my desire...
Sleep Now In The Fire!
    ~ RAGE AGAINST THE MACHINE

December 29

A FREE LUNCH
...is what feeds everyone.

Don't try to tell me
there's no free lunch.
Nearly everyone's first meal
flows freely and lovingly
through their mother's breast.

The price you will pay
for your one and precious life
goes beyond the coin of the realm,
beyond your blood, sweat and tears,
way beyond what you understand
to be your life's objective.

Give with the grace and generosity
Mother Earth gives to you.

Allow the life flowing through you
to pass without exacting a toll.

What you will find worth keeping
moves freely all around you.

And don't ever forget,
the only limitation in life
is your absolute knowing.

Other Voices

*When you get to a place where you understand
that love and belonging, your worthiness,
is a birthright and not something you have to earn,
anything is possible.*
~ Brené Brown

December 30

CLEARHEADED
...and witness to the natural harmony

In a dream state
I hastily scrawled red words
into my black notebook.

But now that I'm awake
I cannot remember
the source of my bitterness,
and I won't allow anger
to write this poem.

Maybe deep sleep is akin
to the eating of a lotus leaf,
that ancient but lost ritual
known as conscious forgetting,
or of allowing the past to pass.

When I refuse to push back,
nothing can push on me.
It simply flows right through.

Other Voices

*Anxiety does not empty tomorrow of its sorrows,
but only empties today of its strength.*
~ CHARLES SPURGEON

December 31

GETTING PAST THE PAST
...slowly, deliberately, with intention

Nothing frightens me more
than the way we live unconsciously,
lost in the shadows of history,
recklessly hurtling through time.

A long life requires special forms
of remembering and forgetting.
But we've mixed them all up.

Memory is not about restoring
some individual, romanticized past,
or holding on to our grudges,
but rather about careful storytelling
to advance life's narrative.

And forgetting is not about becoming
numb to the ways we all suffer
or denying our burdensome past,
but the very conscious letting go
to allow space for new life.

Other Voices

What is past is prologue.
~ William Shakespeare

Acknowledgements

With some sadness, I share that this may be the last daily reader compiled from *Brian's Poem of the Day*. I want to thank my readers for all their support during the years in which I published a daily poem.

The project I humbly titled *Brian's Poem of the Day* began in July 2016. At the outset I really didn't know what to expect or how long it would last. At first, I simply hoped to get through the end of the month. Later I thought perhaps a year. And if you had asked me more recently, I would tell you that my goal was to make it to ten years. Nonetheless, the time has now come for me to turn the page and to slow the production of my writing.

It's difficult to share this news with my daily readers. Many have been along for the ride since the beginning. And I'd be remiss if I didn't share how grateful I am to those who've helped me immensely with their feedback and with preparing my books for publication. I love to write but editing and publishing can be a grind.

This text is much more polished because of the expert editing provided by Susan Mueller and Jenny Mueller. Yes, they are related to me, but I don't know anyone more qualified as editors who will accept gratitude as payment. And between them they've read enough books to fill a library. I'm in awe of their understanding and appreciation for language and literature.

And without a doubt, I've been working with the best book designer for several years now. Adam Robinson is an author in his own right, but he's also a virtuoso when it comes to design and publishing. I only wish Adam didn't live so far away, as I'd like to share an office with him. (I'm sure he'd never allow it.) Be sure to check out Adam's work at GoodBookDevelopers.com.

Finally, if you've been on this spiritual journey right beside me, let's keep on going!

Brian

P.S. – I hope you thoroughly enjoyed my poetry and know this is just one of four volumes of *Brian's Poem of the Day* available for download or purchase. ☺

About Brian

Brian J. Mueller is a poet devoted to finding deeper meaning and beauty through seeking spirituality in community with others. He lives and works in Dayton, Ohio and practices writing poetry daily. Whenever possible he comes together with others seeking understanding through open and honest sharing of life experiences. Among Brian's poetic inspirations are Rumi, Mary Oliver, Mark Nepo, Charles Bukowski, Wendell Berry, and his dog Simon.

Though Brian spends his days providing website design and management, most mornings begin with a cup of tea and devoting a little bit of time to both reading and meditating. His dog Simon cheerfully keeps him company and inspires him to continue his efforts. Despite the fact writing poetry has helped him glimpse a much larger universe, Brian still enjoys staying close to home where he can enjoy local gatherings and spend time with his wife Melissa.

*If a thing loves,
it is infinite.*
~ WILLIAM BLAKE

Also by Brian J. Mueller

2002	2015	2016	2017
Bull Head	**Bull Heart**	**More Bull**	**Complete Bull**
2017	2018	2019	2020
Tomorrow Could Be Wonderful	**Second Communion**	**Jonah**	**The Invitation**

More information is available at *www.BriansPoems.com*.
You can find these books at online retailers or order them through your favorite bookstore!

Notes

These pages are for your thoughts and poems…

Made in the USA
Columbia, SC
16 February 2021